Home Lighting Ideas

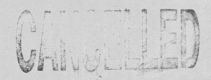

Home Lighting Ideas

AURA
EDITIONS

Author: Richard Wiles
Editor: Barry Milton
Designers: Jonathan Lambert,
            Keith Faulkner

Published by Aura Editions
2 Derby Road, Greenford, Middlesex

Produced by Marshall Cavendish Books Limited
58 Old Compton Street, London W1V 5PA

© Marshall Cavendish Limited 1985

ISBN 0 86307 444 8

Typesetting and make-up by Quadraset Limited,
Midsomer Norton, Bath, Avon

Printed and bound by Jerez Industrial S.A. Spain

Contents

Introduction

A well-planned lighting scheme adds the finishing touch to your room's decor — and in hard-working areas such as the kitchen and study, sensibly-placed lights are a practical necessity to prevent eye strain and accidents. Unfortunately, the lighting circuitry of most homes is designed with a virtual disregard for the niceties of good sense: the token light installed when the house was built (or when the system was put into an older property) is invariably a pendant dangling from the centre of the ceiling in the misguided belief that overall light is best. The most adventurous set-up you're likely to find is one offering wall lights.

You needn't baulk at the thought of tampering with your house's electrical system: with a lot of patience — and a determination to follow sensible procedures and comply with the legalities — you'll find that adapting your lighting system to produce the effects you want is quite straightforward.

Lighting design relies a lot on aesthetics — what looks nice — but your choice of a particular set-up should be influenced by a sound back-up knowledge of what's possible technically. Here's where the Book of Home Lighting Ideas can help you: not only does it give a thorough grounding in lighting options on a room-by-room basis, but also it doubles as a concise textbook of skills, presented in step-by-step format, which will enable you to tackle any job from fitting a plug on a newly acquired table lamp to installing two-way switching in your hall and landing.

CHAPTER 1
Planning better lighting

Artificial lighting should primarily be functional — allowing you to find your way round the house at night or enabling you to read without straining your eyes — while at the same time it should decoratively suggest subtle or lively moods, as you deem suitable.

The type of effect you create hinges largely on the fitting — and the type of bulb it uses — which you choose to illuminate a particular area. Its position, however, is probably the most influential factor. The most complementary balance between light and dark is crucial: heavy shadows can be imposing, whereas uniformly bright lighting can seem stark and clinical.

To ensure a good blend of tones without hard, dark patches, aim to provide a modest backdrop of light throughout a room and use local lights to give extra illumination where it's needed — to highlight an attractive feature such as a fireplace or group of pictures, for instance, or to provide sufficient light to read by comfortably.

One important design point you should take into account when working out your lighting schemes is to ensure that naked light bulbs aren't visible to anyone sitting or standing in the room to avoid dazzling. You can usually fulfil this basic requirement with the style of fitting you buy — low level lights generally have shades to hide the bulb, whereas rise-and-fall pendants solve the problem over a dining table.

Work through the following room-by-room guide to scheming, then make sketch plans on site to indicate where you want light in relation to furniture and other features, before discovering in the following chapters just how electricity is not so daunting as you fear.

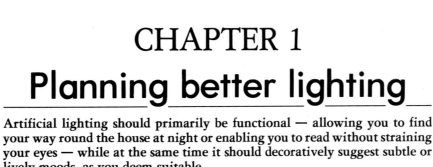

Living room

The living room is typically a place for relaxation, so lighting should be conducive to leisure activities such as reading, watching TV — perhaps dabbling with a hobby, knitting, sewing or just listening to music.

For practicality, avoid just a central ceiling pendant in the living room: it seldom casts sufficient light on its own to reach all the corners. You'll also find that the page of a book or newspaper you're reading is annoyingly cast in shadow and a strain to read.

People being fickle, you can't expect to exist in the same mood constantly, so don't settle on just one lighting scheme for your living room — incorporate adaptable features when you arrange the fittings, so the atmosphere can be calm and lulling when you're tired after a hard

Subdued lighting provided by decorative table lamps lends a relaxed, cosy air to this living room

A single pendant light in the living room is unlikely to provide suitable all-round illumination

A spotlight aimed at an area of seating will dazzle anyone trying to read, casting the page in shadow

day's work, or bright and breezy when you're entertaining.

Spotlights on track systems fixed to the ceiling or wall at the perimeter — preferably not the centre — of the room allow you to angle the individual lamps where you like. Aim them at a bookshelf, display case or plain wall; or use them as reading lamps. But never aim them directly at an area of seating — they'll tend to give the impression that anyone sitting there is on stage.

Wall lights are a useful addition to a living room scheme but you must place them at the right height where they won't dazzle anyone sitting, yet where they'll not look too low or high when standing next to them. Place a wall light centrally within the length of wall, or equally spaced if two or more are used.

Never underestimate the versatility of the dimmer switch in your lighting plans — most of the fittings in your living room are suitable for dimming to vary the effect of their output and alter the atmosphere.

Easy on the eyes

Position a reading lamp — preferably one which can be adjusted easily — directly behind your chair to illuminate whatever tome you're reading. For more subtle illumination without the risk of glare, a table or standard lamp placed behind you allows you to read (or knit) without straining your eyes.

For sewing or other intricate work, you'll require a brighter light, and a spotlight mounted on the wall behind the chair, or freestanding and adjustable on a track or standard is ideal. Don't position spotlights so they point directly at a seating area opposite.

Reducing TV contrast

A television tends to dominate a room, partly because of the sound and the action on the screen, but largely because of the glare from the tube. Lighting in a room where there's a frequently-watched TV set should be designed to reduce the overall glare with judiciously placed low-level fittings nearby. A table or standard lamp behind or to one side of the set will lessen the effect of the flickering screen (but never place a lamp directly on top of the set; it's a positive fire risk should overheating occur). Alcove or shelf lamps concealed by a baffle can also provide gentle background illumination without vying with the TV.

Washing the walls

Wallwasher fittings can create dramatically stylish effects by flooding a wall with light, and so indirectly illuminating the rest of the room. Using reflector floods, graded washes in decreasing wattages are possible for a less flamboyant effect, while downlighters fitted to the ceiling can be used to create scalloped washes or gentle curves of light. It's a method ideally suited to a plain, uninterrupted wall that's free from obstructions which would cause harsh shadows.

Sensible sites for switches

Don't neglect the importance of an easily-located switch or switches to control your lighting. The standard set-up is by the door to the room, but consider two-way switching versatility, perhaps locating another switch at the opposite side of the room, or at the entrance to an adjoining room.

Table lamps, standard lamps and other local fittings usually have their own integral switches, but consider centralizing their operation with a conveniently-placed bank of socket outlets. Make sure that you fit a switched socket outlet.

The best position for a reading lamp is directly behind the sitter, when the page will be illuminated

A table lamp will help to diffuse the constant flickering from a television set, which can cause eye strain

An uplighter will also help to provide a general level of light that will lessen the television glare

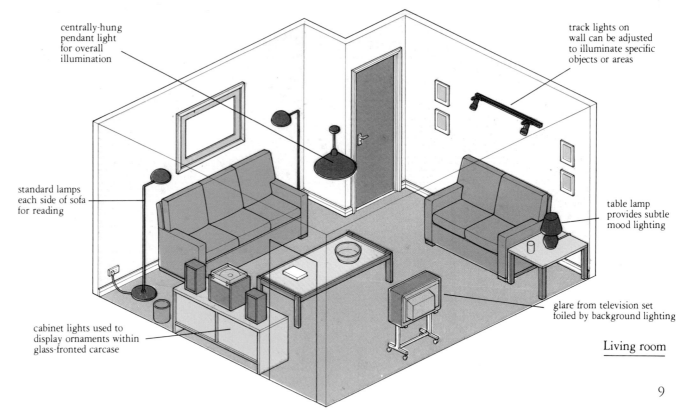

centrally-hung pendant light for overall illumination

track lights on wall can be adjusted to illuminate specific objects or areas

standard lamps each side of sofa for reading

table lamp provides subtle mood lighting

cabinet lights used to display ornaments within glass-fronted carcase

glare from television set foiled by background lighting

Living room

9

Dining room

The dining room creates its own special problems when planning a lighting scheme, in that the table needs its own source of illumination without dazzling those eating, while the rest of the room needs to be lit at the same time.

Because people generally sit facing each other across the dining table, lights fitted at one side or the other will tend to cast shadows across the table or glare at diners opposite. This means that wall lights are really quite impractical, except merely for subdued background lighting. Spotlights are definitely out unless you're so proud of your culinary skills that you want to highlight the contents of everybody's plate.

Unlike other rooms, the best type of fitting for the dining room is a central

A pendant lamp with a baffle shade is ideal for the dining table

A single pendant light over the dining table will dazzle diners sitting opposite if it's too low

Spotlights above and behind diners will either dazzle those opposite or cast their faces in shadow

pendant light. The lamp, though, should not be strung so high that the lighting it gives is cold and stark, or so low that sitters find they're staring straight at a lampshade or, even worse, a bare bulb.

Light and height
Rise-and-fall fittings (see page 52) are a good choice for over-table lighting: there are many styles, from the traditional 'lantern' types on exposed pulleys to modern versions with the working parts sealed from view (which also usually incorporate a bulbous shade to conceal the bulb and filter the light).

Adjustable pendants such as these can be pulled down low over the table and the light level controlled by a dimmer switch for more intimate meals, or raised and brightened for day-to-day dining, or when the table's not in use.

On a long table, two rise-and-fall fittings are best, so there's constant light for the entire surface.

On the table
Apart from decorative, romantic effects possible with simple candles in holders, you can use other, electrical fittings on the table itself for a warm, atmospheric air while dining. Oil lamp style fittings, commonly with glass globe shades and brass bodies, look stylish when perched in the centre of a table — but not blocking the view of two people sitting opposite — so long as the flex can be run safely to the socket outlet. This is probably only a feasible idea where the dining table is next to a wall. Then the flex can be draped over the edge of the table and run along to a socket clear of the feet of anybody sitting at the table.

10

See to serve

The table is not the only part of the dining room that needs to be lit: serving areas such as a sideboard, or a hatchway in the wall from the kitchen require their share, too. This light should be direct — so you can see what to dish out — but localized and subdued to prevent a conflict with the table arrangement. Downlighters, wallwashers or eyeball fittings (see page 50), recessed into the ceiling at the perimeter of the room, offer this delicate but practical level of illumination, and should be independently-switched from the other, main room lighting.

Perimeter lights concealed behind a pelmet and shining down onto a curtain will create a gentle overall room light where more direct lighting is also in use over the table.

Table lamps, too, can suggest an intimate light conducive to relaxed dinner parties.

For the living/dining area

In a through room, where dining is allocated one half, it's wise to plan the lighting to that the living and eating sections are separately lit and controlled respectively — but go for an arrangement that allows both schemes to complement each other, perhaps blending. Too harsh a light in the living area will counteract any subtle illumination you want for the dining room, whereas a dimly-lit dining area can suggest a cold, dull patch from a cosy living room.

Electrical alternatives

Of course, there's no reason why you should have to be limited to electricity when arranging artificial lighting schemes: don't underestimate the value of candles and oil lamps. A well-laid table lit by a flickering flame creates an intimate mood for entertaining.

A rise-and-fall pendant light can be adjusted in height to suit the mood and avoid dazzling diners

Over a long dining table you'll probably need two rise-and-fall lights to avoid the furthest reaches being kept in the dark

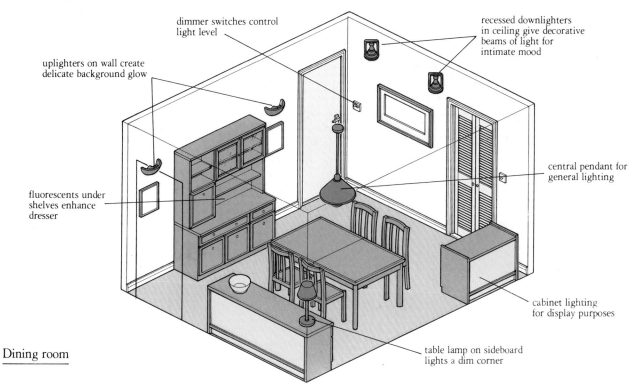

dimmer switches control light level

recessed downlighters in ceiling give decorative beams of light for intimate mood

uplighters on wall create delicate background glow

fluorescents under shelves enhance dresser

central pendant for general lighting

cabinet lighting for display purposes

table lamp on sideboard lights a dim corner

Dining room

Kitchen

Primarily a place of work, the kitchen needs good efficient lighting to illuminate the main task areas — cooker, worktops and sink — but you must choose fittings with care to avoid creating a wholly utilitarian atmosphere in the room.

Poor lighting is responsible for many accidents in the kitchen, so your priority should be to provide practical lighting over the work areas, which won't cast shadows over the shoulder.

Task lighting for work areas

By far the most efficient solution for kitchen lighting is to fit tungsten or fluorescent tubes, concealing them under the lower edge of wall units, behind baffles to prevent glare: in this way the light is directed downwards just where it's needed, which is an important factor to consider when you're using sharp implements for food preparation.

Track and spotlights installed over the sink or work areas can also be successful, but only where the beams thrown out won't dazzle you from another point in the room — this could be a danger if you're carrying a hot pan. Don't aim a spotlight at the sink, for instance, if it means you'll be standing in front of your own shadow when washing up.

All appliances should be well lit: a cooker hood typically includes an integral light, which can be used over the hob, whereas the sink, washing machine and dishwasher can be illuminated with spotlight or downlighter beams trained on them. The refrigerator has its own integral light, so it doesn't need additional illumination unless its top doubles as a work surface.

Background details

You'll need some form of general light in

addition to the localized pools over work surfaces and appliances. If the kitchen is fairly small, a single, ceiling-mounted fluorescent strip could provide the correct level of light, although close-fitting bowl type fittings (see page 40) are a good choice because they're easy to keep clean in the potentially greasy atmosphere of a kitchen.

Illuminate the ceiling

Fluorescents do tend to offer the best, contrast-free lighting for practical areas such as the kitchen, but the fittings can look rather clinical. One way of solving this problem is to install an illuminated ceiling — in effect lowering the height of the room with translucent panels fixed in a lightweight frame.

The fluorescent tubes themselves are fixed to the ceiling as normal, and hidden behind the panels, which can be plain, coloured or textured — their light shines through, creating a glowing surface with all the benefits of an ordinary tube.

Fluorescents can be wired in banks to provide even illumination across the area of the ceiling, or you can include a solid margin around the translucent parts into which you can recess downlighters or eyeball fittings for directing light onto work surfaces or the breakfast bar, as shown in the photograph above.

For the kitchen-diner

If you eat in your kitchen, a rise-and-fall fitting (see page 52) installed over the table can provide temporary, independently-switched subtle light in place of the practical fluorescent effect while you eat. If you've an island bar unit, install downlighters directly above for best light during a meal.

The basic downlighter fitting can be equipped with a variety of different lamps to either focus or spread the light.

A single central pendant light is useless in a practical area like the kitchen where work surfaces are positioned around the outsides: you'd be working in your own shadow at cooker or worktop

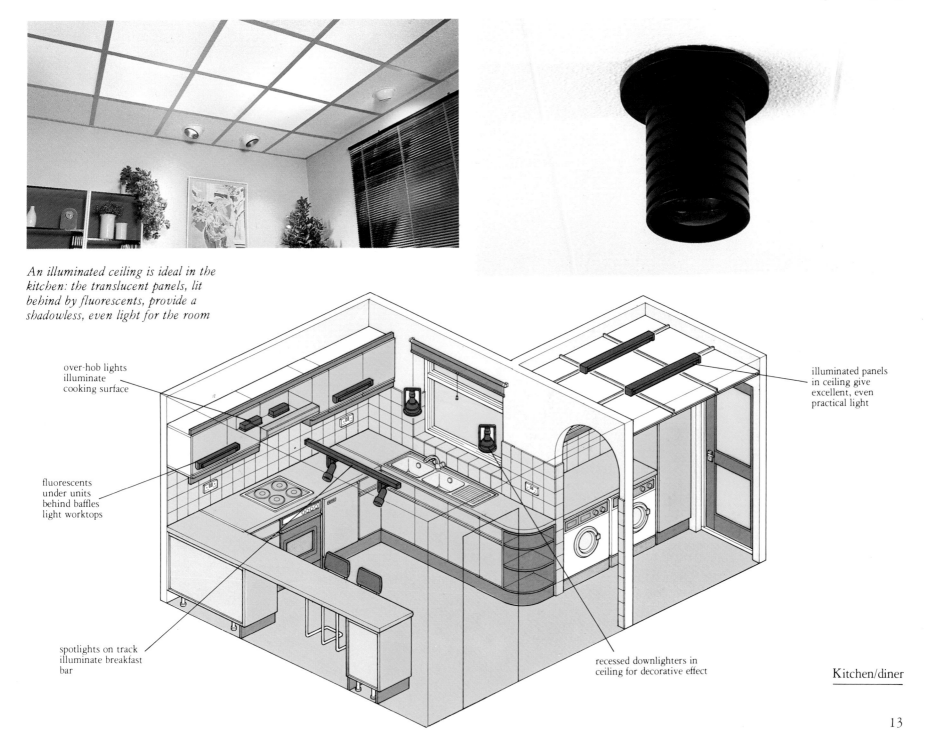

An illuminated ceiling is ideal in the kitchen: the translucent panels, lit behind by fluorescents, provide a shadowless, even light for the room

over-hob lights illuminate cooking surface

fluorescents under units behind baffles light worktops

spotlights on track illuminate breakfast bar

recessed downlighters in ceiling for decorative effect

illuminated panels in ceiling give excellent, even practical light

Kitchen/diner

13

Bedrooms

Bedroom lighting should be restful, but you'll also need to allow provision for reading between the covers, dressing and perhaps making up. If you have children, their domain often requires special attention during the dark hours.

You'll rarely need any provision for bright lighting schemes in a bedroom, so concentrate on creating a relaxing set-up of subtle pools of light set against a modest background illumination, perhaps provided by a central ceiling pendant operated by a dimmer switch. Perimeter lighting can offer some gentle effects on the walls.

Curling up with a good book

Bedhead or bedside lights, operated by two-way switches, are a must to save you having to nip from between the sheets when you want to switch the light on or off at night — ideally you'll need a switch by the door and one at each side of a double bed (see page 45).

Two directional lights in a shared bedroom are useful if one person wants to sleep while the other reads. Most people read in bed lying propped up on the pillows, so the best location for a reading light is on the wall or bedhead above your head, or on a beside table.

A night light for the children

Many kids prefer the security of sleeping in a room when there's a light on — but there's no need to leave a powerful bulb burning all night. Either fit a dimmer switch to reduce the output (and incidentally, the consumption of electricity), or leave the door ajar and light the room indirectly from a lower-wattage bulb in the adjoining hall or landing.

Purpose-made night lights intended for safe use in children's rooms are available, and you can perch them at the cot-side or at the other side of the room — it's also a boon if you have to rise at night to tend to a hungry baby (switching on a bright light when your eyes are still in slumberland can be quite a shock).

Lighting cupboards and wardrobes

Fitted wardrobes or storage units in a bedroom can be fairly deep, dark places where you could easily lose a favourite item of clothing. Internal lighting, operated when the doors are opened, is a benefit here, allowing you to locate what you want without having to resort to a torch.

Fix striplights above the inner face of the door frame, or at the sides if there are shelves that would otherwise be cast in shadow. Special automatic cupboard lights (see page 30) are available to save

Independently-switched and dimmed lights at bedside give a subtle glow

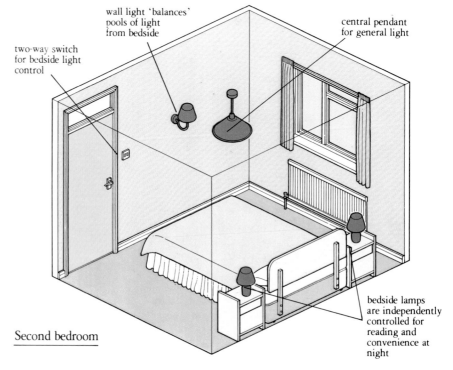

wall light 'balances' pools of light from bedside

central pendant for general light

two-way switch for bedside light control

bedside lamps are independently controlled for reading and convenience at night

Second bedroom

you having to grope for a switch.

Reflective lighting
If your bedroom includes a vanity unit or dressing mirror you'll certainly need good lighting to check that you come up to muster — even in the daytime some sort of make-up light is an asset. Light should ideally shine on your face, not on the mirror, so table lamps or striplights at each side of the mirror (or above it, for that matter) will give a good balance, preventing glare.

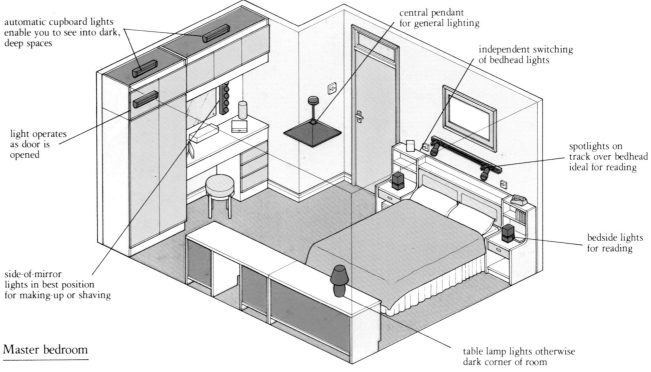

automatic cupboard lights enable you to see into dark, deep spaces

central pendant for general lighting

independent switching of bedhead lights

light operates as door is opened

spotlights on track over bedhead ideal for reading

side-of-mirror lights in best position for making-up or shaving

bedside lights for reading

table lamp lights otherwise dark corner of room

Master bedroom

An ornate bedside lamp can be fitted with a shade to match your bedroom

Decorative screens can help to diffuse bright lights in a bedroom. Place them in front of large table lamps or spotlights

A light fixed above the bedhead is excellent for sitting up and reading and should have an integral switch

A nightlight in a young child's or baby's room will provide the comfort and security that's needed

15

Workroom

If you use part of your home as a study, or the kids have been allocated a quiet corner for pondering over their homework, you'll appreciate the benefit of an efficient lighting set-up that doesn't turn the house into a fully-fledged office complex.

Good lighting is essential if you're studying documents, writing a great deal or calculating the home accounts. There are numerous types of desk lamps available, in a range of traditionally decorative and modern streamlined styles, all of which can usually be angled as required to cast a pool of light on the page — most types use a maximum 60W light bulb, which gives clear but not over-bright illumination that's best for reading.

The best angle

The best angle for the light from a desk lamp is not necessarily directed straight at the paper you're working on: if the paper is very shiny, it will reflect the light and dazzle you. Adjustable lamps are meant to be manoeuvred, so swivel and tilt it until you achieve the level of light that doesn't strain your eyes unduly. Often it's best to direct the beam at a wall or part of the desk to one side of the paper, and work by the indirect light.

Covering all options

Don't position a reading lamp behind you: you'll only be working in your own shadow. If you have a desk with a fold-down flap, you can achieve a good level of constant light by fitting an automatic cabinet light — with a fluorescent or tungsten strip fitting — in the top edge of the desk, so that the beam floods the desk surface.

Where you are likely to use a typewriter, an adjustable desk lamp with a long arm is best. Place it behind or to one side of the typewriter and bring the lamp head directly over the keyboard, and very slightly forward, so that the keys are illuminated and the typing head and paper aren't in shadow.

Home computer buffs should adopt the same principal for the computer, but only indirectly light the monitor (or TV) screen to avoid irritating reflections — many purpose-made displays for computers include a brilliance control for night or day use.

A little general light

Staring at printed matter for a long time in the isolated beam of a desk lamp can be very tiring on the eyes, so it's important to include some general background lighting for the workroom. A central ceiling pendant is probably the best choice here, fitted with a dimmer switch for greater flexibility.

A clip-on desk lamp adjusts to light just the area you're working on

A light behind a desk will mean you'll be working in your own shadow

A single ceiling pendant casts the same shadows over the desktop

A desk lamp with a long, adjustable arm can be angled precisely so as to illuminate the page or the book

Reposition the lamp directly over a typewriter so the keys and type head won't be cast in shadow

For intricate work

If your workroom is a place where you're involved in more intricate work, such as assembling electronic devices, model-making or another fiddly hobby, more workmanlike utility lighting is necessary. Rig up a work surface along a wall and fit fluorescent striplights underneath an overhanging shelf to give you a blanket of shadowless illumination. You may even need more direct light for tackling minute details, in the form of a small spotlight — you can buy miniature types which clip onto a shelf or desktop so that you can move them to any position along the back edge of the work surface.

Attic, halls, stairs & landings

Whether your attic is used only to store boxes of household treasures and unfashionable artefacts you'd rather not dispose of, or whether it's a loft conversion providing an extra room, you'll need to consider a successful lighting arrangement.

A loft conversion should be treated as for any other room in the house, following the guidelines laid down for whatever room it's to become. Consider, however, the likelihood that the room's shape will be unconventional, due to the slope of the room in which it's set. A centrally-hung pendant, then, may brightly light the top of the 'triangle' but the parts at the base may be dimly lit. Wall lights are probably impracticable, due to the sloping ceiling, unless they are the bulkhead or close-fitting ceiling types, which wouldn't look out of place at an odd angle.

Table lamps, standard lamps and track-lights are probably your best choice, as you can fit them into irregular corners — they'll also provide dramatic or decoratively-shaped pools of light which can enhance the shape of the room.

A loft for storage
If you use the loft infrequently for storage, a single light bulb strung high in the ridge of the roof will provide general light to most of the void, although it will be difficult to avoid shadows when you're looking for anything.

If you don't want to go to the trouble of connecting the attic to the main lighting system, you'll be able to make do with a portable inspection lamp on a long lead, which you can plug into a socket in the room below and carry up into the roof space. Choose a lamp with an integral

hook, which you can hang from a nail driven into a rafter. Other versions incorporate a bulldog-type clip or a clamp, which you can attach to a batten or one of the thinner section roof timbers.

Safety on stairs
Halls, stairs and landings are the few areas of the home where bright lighting is necessary to avoid accidents caused by tripping. But it's still possible to create the mood you want with judicious choice of fittings.

The main requirement is to light all parts of the stairwell, casting beams on

When creeping about in the attic, take a suitable inspection lamp with you so that you can clip it onto a roof timber

the treads of the stairs, with the risers in shadow so they're obvious to the eye. Avoid lights which might dazzle anyone climbing up or down the flight, such as spotlights on the walls.

A pendant or spotlight cluster at the top of a flight is a good choice to light the treads, while at the landing, recessed downlighters or wallwashers can provide more subdued illumination.

In a long hallway, position recessed downlighters or pendants at intervals to produce an overall light level.

Two-way switching between the bottom of a flight and the landing at the top is imperative for safety and convenience (see page 44), and if your house is built on three floors, extend the two-way set-up at the first landing to switch lights on the second landing. Where there is an attic or skylight over the stairs, you can use a suspended ceiling system to make a diffused light for the whole stairway.

A novel idea for lighting a dim stairwell is to fit an illuminated loft hatch for a subtle glow without bright patches

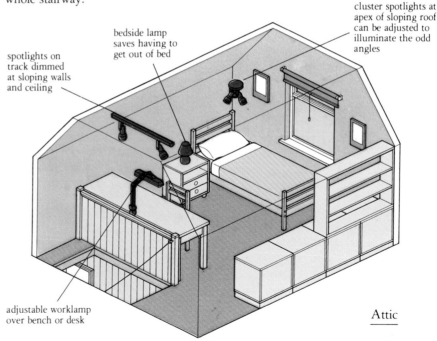

cluster spotlights at apex of sloping roof can be adjusted to illuminate the odd angles

bedside lamp saves having to get out of bed

spotlights on track dimmed at sloping walls and ceiling

adjustable worklamp over bench or desk

Attic

Bathroom & W.C.

The bathroom calls for special lighting arrangements due to the proximity of electricity to water and a steamy environment — the two combined are lethal.

Electrical wiring regulations forbid the use of socket outlets and conventional switches in the bathroom, as there's a danger from shock where anyone with wet hands operates an electrical appliance. Switches must be pull-cord operated and light fittings must be of the enclosed type. Ordinary ceiling roses must be replaced with batten holders.

Many bathrooms in modern houses or flats have no windows, so you've plenty of scope for adventurous lighting design — it will be used whenever anyone enters the bathroom, day or night. Many people opt for a low light level as it suggests a calm, relaxed atmosphere ideal for soaking in a bath-tub. Recessed downlighters can give a relaxing, subtle illumination for the bathroom, whereas striplights are too clinical.

Mirrors are used as much as the bathroom fittings, so aim for a good practical light arrangement here. Avoid an over-mirror light, which casts a shadow over your face, making it awkward to apply make-up properly, or shave successfully. Lights should be fixed at one or both sides of the mirror for even illumination. Bathroom striplights, some of which include a shaver outlet, are a good choice.

If you have a shower cubicle you'll probably need a light to shine inside — special shower lights, which are totally enclosed against steam and moisture, fit closely to the ceiling above the cubicle.

An ideal bathroom arrangement of overhead and side-mirror lights

Don't use an over-mirror light; it will cast unflattering shadows over your face as you make-up or shave

Lights at the side of a mirror — like theatrical dressing-room types — offer even, shadow-free illumination

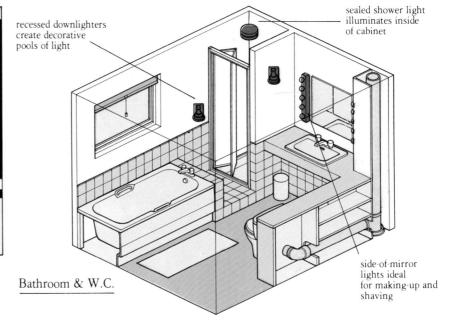

recessed downlighters create decorative pools of light

sealed shower light illuminates inside of cabinet

side-of-mirror lights ideal for making-up and shaving

Bathroom & W.C.

Porch & house exterior

Illuminate the entrance to your house both for security against prowlers and to give guests a welcoming light to find their way to your door. And if you're keen on summer evening parties outdoors, why not set the mood with decorative garden lighting?

A proper weatherproof exterior light is best for illuminating your front door, not only deterring prospective thieves but also shining a light for guests to locate your house in the dark.

Various styles of fitting are available, typically the traditional lantern-types or modern bulkhead fittings, which offer a more functional look. The lights should be switched conveniently from just inside the door. Don't make the mistake of fitting too high a bulb wattage: even a low-watt bulb will be sufficient.

If you have an enclosed porch, you have more choice of fittings, as it's not necessary to stick to sealed exterior fittings — other types are made which can be fitted in a semi-enclosed situation.

For a house with a striking feature such as an architecturally-interesting façade, exterior spotlights fitted either on the wall itself, on part of an adjoining structure or at ground level can enhance the feature at night.

If your house has a long drive or path, which is shielded by trees or shrubs, you'd be wise to fit lights along its length for security against prowlers and to guide legitimate callers to your door.

Typical outside lights include bollard fittings, which are set in the ground along the edge of a path or drive to illuminate its route. Spotlights with ground spikes are an alternative for more direct

lighting. Gate lights, switched from the house, are a boon here too. Lantern-style fittings are made for a traditional look.

It's a good idea to fit a wall light high on a corner of the house, too, to prevent anyone sneaking unnoticed to a side gate.

Brighten up the night-time garden

Barbecues and bonfire parties will go off with greater success if your guests can see what they're eating, and in addition to the outdoor lighting already mentioned, which is mainly practical, you should also include temporary illumination with a decorative lilt effect.

Low-voltage lighting kits allow you to string coloured lanterns and bulbs from the trees, bushes, along fences and around the house, for a truly party atmosphere — and without any danger from electricity.

A lantern-style wall light makes an impressive show on a porch exterior

More practical — ideal for garden lighting — tough bulkhead fittings

Neat adjustable spotlights on ground spikes can be used to light a drive

Porch lights can be very decorative and enchance your house frontage

19

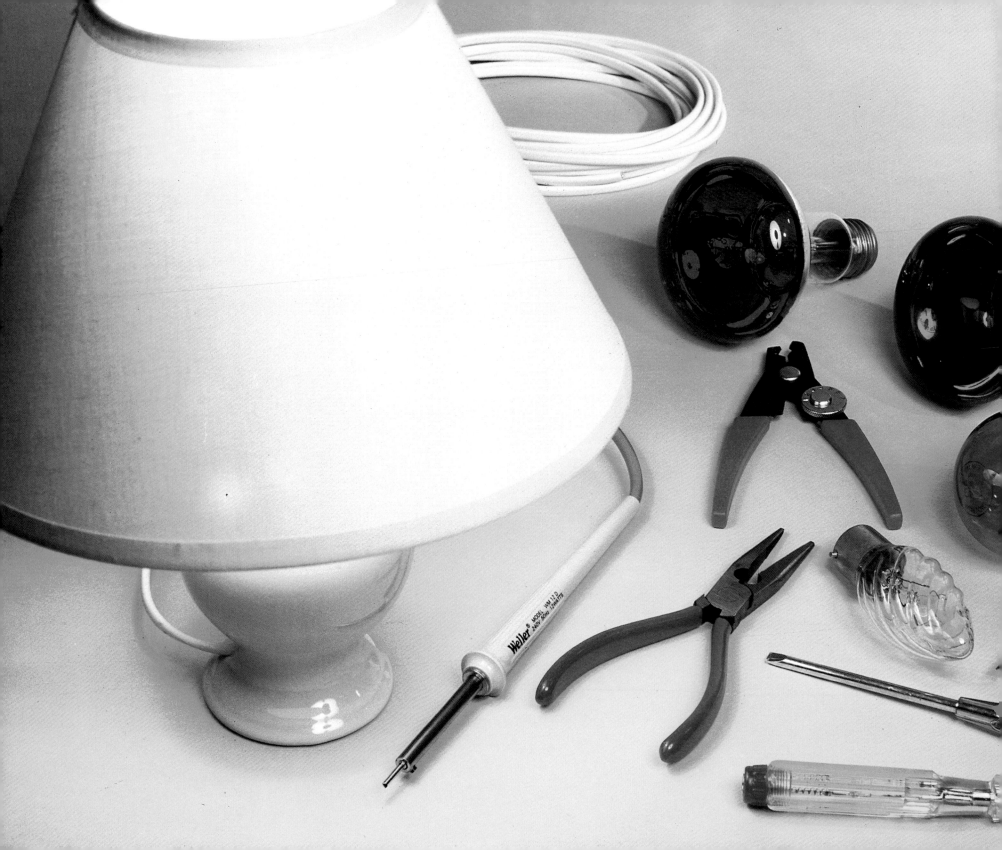

CHAPTER 2
Lighting basics

There are numerous ways you can put into practice your lighting schemes without being an expert electrician. What's required is an understanding of how your electrical system works. Electricity basically reaches your house through one thick 'service cable', passing through a 'service fuse' and into the meter. Modern electrical installations comprise two wires — the live and neutral 'meter tails' — which carry the power to the 'consumer unit': this is where the power is sub-divided into 'circuits' for lighting and power. Each circuit is fitted with its own 'fuse': this works on the principle that wire heats up when electricity passes through it; if the wire overheats, it melts. Electrical circuits work on the same basic principle by which a battery powers a torch bulb: connect a wire to the positive (+) terminal and another to the negative (−) terminal and join the two ends to a bulb and electricity will flow from positive to negative along them. The difference with a house's power circuit is that the electricity flows, not in one direction, but in both directions. Consider 'positive' as 'live', 'negative' as 'neutral'. Earthing is provided for safety throughout the electrical installation — it's connected to the metal parts of switches, sockets and other accessories so that in the event of a fault electricity will flow along it to blow a fuse. Cables are used to carry the electricity around the house in a single casing: they comprise the copper wires that form live and neutral 'cores' and are encased in PVC insulation to prevent them from touching. The cores are wrapped in a PVC sheath.

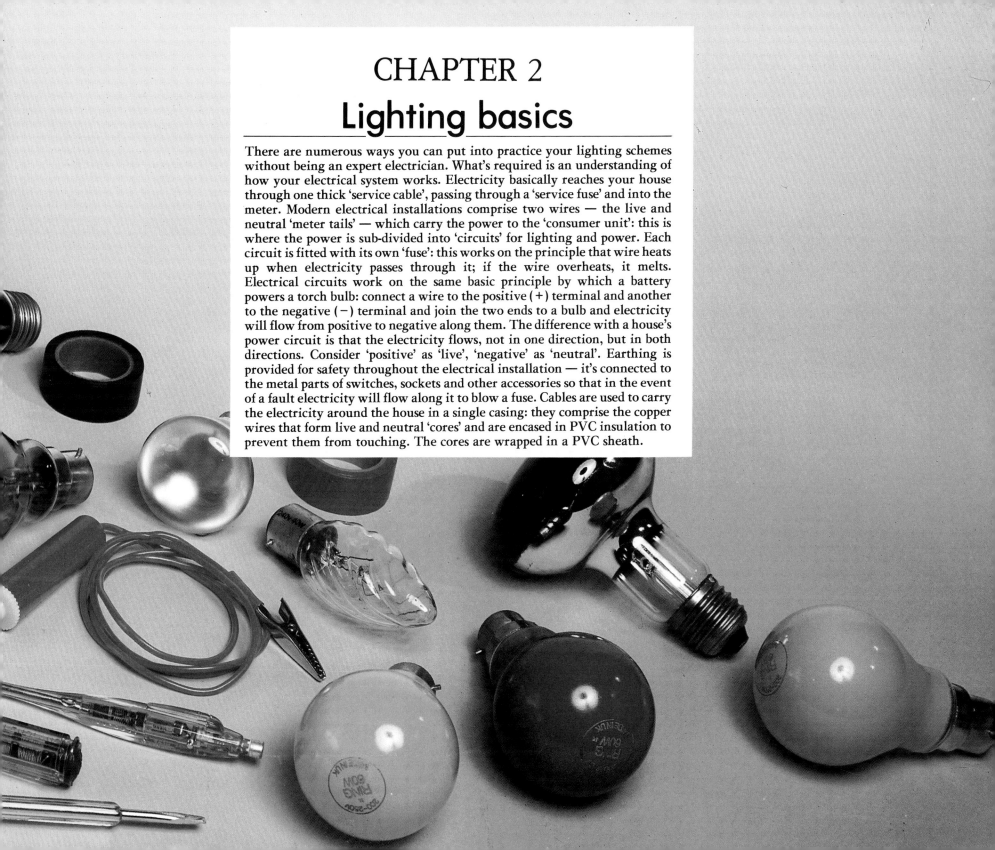

Power circuits

You don't just use the lighting circuits to illuminate your home: the power circuits, too, are used for table lamps, standard lamps and other portable fittings. Often, there's an insufficiency of socket outlets, or existing ones are inconveniently placed: understand how they're arranged in the system and you'll be able to modify the set-up.

There are basically two types of power circuits you're likely to find in your home: 'radials' and 'rings'. The former, which in older systems was the sole means of wiring power circuits, is still in use today for special situations; the latter, installed since about 1960, is now the most commonly used, and more versatile set-up which can cope with more sockets than a radial installation.

1 Radial circuits These comprise a single cable, which leaves the fuse box and runs on to one or more socket outlets. Take a look at the cables emerging from the circuit fusecarriers in your fuse box: a radial circuit is denoted by one live (red) cable core.

Older homes needed fewer sockets than we tend to find use for today, due to the proliferation of appliances and fittings available. The sockets — round-holed to take round-pin plugs -- were rated at 2, 5 or 15A and were fed by rubber- or lead-sheathed cable. This deteriorates with age and should be examined by a qualified electrician, as it's unlikely to cope with the demands of a modern household. Re-wiring is nearly always advisable.

Radial circuits are still used in modern systems, where a ring circuit would be uneconomical in use of cable (feeding a socket outlet in a remote part of the building, for example), to take power to single major appliances — such as the cooker or an instantaneous shower — or to an outbuilding. A radial circuit can have any number of sockets.

The Wiring Regulations demand that a radial circuit serving a floor area up to 50sq m (538sq ft) must be run in 4mm² cable and protected by a 30A cartridge fuse or MCB. For a floor area up to 20sq m (215sq ft) a radial circuit must be run in 2.5mm² and be protected by a 20A fuse or MCB.

2 Ring circuits Starting and finishing at the consumer unit, a ring circuit is, as its name suggests, a loop, with socket outlets inserted along its length. Examine your circuit fuse-carriers at the consumer unit: two live (red) cores emerging from each fuse way indicates that your house is wired with ring circuits.

Current flows around the circuit in both directions to the socket in use — as you're likely to want to use all the sockets at once, the chances of an overload are minimal, so you can have as many sockets as you like on the ring. The circuit, however, mustn't serve an area of more than 100sq m (1076sq ft). It must be wired in 2.5mm² cable and be protected by a 30A fuse or MCB. It can supply a maximum of 7200W.

The number of socket outlets on a ring circuit can be increased by adding branches, called spurs: these single cables can be connected to the main circuit via a junction box or to the terminals of any socket on the ring main. You can fit one spur to each existing socket and end up with either a single or a double outlet.

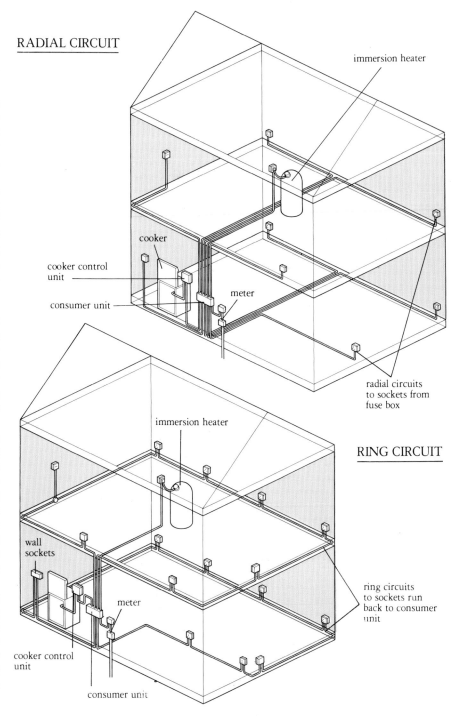

RADIAL CIRCUIT

immersion heater

cooker

cooker control unit

consumer unit

meter

radial circuits to sockets from fuse box

RING CIRCUIT

immersion heater

wall sockets

meter

cooker control unit

consumer unit

ring circuits to sockets run back to consumer unit

Lighting circuits

Your house lighting circuits will be wired in one of two ways, or a combination of the two. It is important to be able to identify which system is which, so that alterations can be safely and easily carried out with minimum fuss and disruption.

Generally, houses have one lighting circuit serving the downstairs lights and a separate one serving fittings upstairs. They're usually set out as 'radial' circuits, where a cable leaves the consumer unit or distribution box (where power enters the house and is divided into separate circuits), and feeds a light fitting.

Switching on and off

So that each light on the circuit can be independently controlled without preventing the flow of electricity to the next lighting point, it's necessary to install a switch that will break the live core of that cable, so turning off the light. There are basically two ways this can be done:

1 Junction box system The older method, which can be wasteful of cable, but which is still used occasionally, comprises a cable that leaves the consumer unit and is connected to a series of four-terminal junction (or joint) boxes. A second cable runs from each box to the terminals of the lighting point — normally the ceiling rose, to which the lampholder is connected by a length of flexible cord (flex) — and a third wire runs to the terminals of the light switch.

The junction box method is especially useful when fitting wall lights, where there is usually restricted space behind the fitting for the connections.

The junction box system, however, is

rather wasteful of lengths of cable.

Additions to the junction box system are possible by inserting another junction box in the power cable and running cables to the new lighting points and the lighting switches.

2 Loop-in system The second, more modern — and economical — method of providing lighting uses special loop-in ceiling roses, which have extra terminals, instead of junction boxes: the cable stemming from the consumer unit enters a rose, then loops out to the next rose on the circuit and so on, to terminate at the furthest rose on the circuit. A second cable takes the power to a switch and back up through the light itself.

Additions to the lighting circuit (see page 36) are possible by connecting a branch cable into the loop-in ceiling rose: four cables are provided for.

How many bulbs are allowed?

A 5 amp (A) fuse or miniature circuit breaker (MCB) in the consumer unit protects modern lighting circuits, which are wired in either 1.0mm^2 or 1.5mm^2 cable (see page 24). This means that each circuit is able to supply up to 1200 watts — that's about twelve lampholders containing 100W bulbs (or smaller wattages).

However, it is likely that you will want to fit bulbs which have higher wattages, and this restricts the circuits to only eight lighting points. Because of this, separate circuits are required for each floor of the house: in a large house, several may be called for. This is sensible, too, meaning that should a fuse in the consumer unit blow, the entire house is not thrown into total darkness.

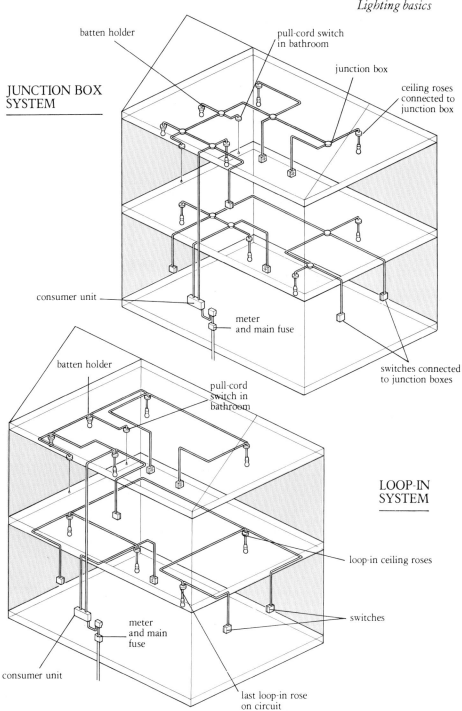

JUNCTION BOX SYSTEM

batten holder

pull-cord switch in bathroom

junction box

ceiling roses connected to junction box

consumer unit

meter and main fuse

switches connected to junction boxes

batten holder

pull-cord switch in bathroom

LOOP-IN SYSTEM

loop-in ceiling roses

switches

consumer unit

meter and main fuse

last loop-in rose on circuit

Flex, cables & lamps

A circuit isn't a circuit without cable to carry the power to fixed accessories and flex to connect light fittings and portable appliances to the fixed wiring. And when it comes to producing light, you'll be in the dark without a suitable lamp.

Cable for fixed wiring

Cable is the fixed part of the domestic electrical system that is normally hidden under the plaster. It runs between the consumer unit and all the fixed outlets and appliances.

Two-core and earth cable has three copper cores, two sheathed in colour-coded PVC — red for live; black for neutral — and the third, the earth core, is bare. In loop-in lighting circuits, the red and the black cores are both live so the black must be flagged.

The three cores are covered with a thick PVC outer sheath, usually flat in profile (grey for burial in walls; white for surface-mounting). When this outer sheath is stripped off, the uninsulated earth core must be sleeved.

Three-core and earth cable is used in two-way switching (see page 44). It has cores insulated in red, blue and yellow PVC, with an uninsulated earth core.

Cable is supplied in metric sizes, referring to the cross-sectional area of the conductors. The most common sizes for lighting circuits are 1.0mm² and 1.5mm²; for ring main, 2.5mm².

Flex for connecting appliances

Flexible cord or 'flex', is used to connect appliances to the fixed wiring. It is round in section and there are various types.

Three-core flex contains three cores (each several strands of copper) in colour-coded PVC insulation: brown for live; blue for neutral; green/yellow striped for earth. All cores are sheathed in white or coloured PVC. It's used in 1.0mm² and 1.5mm² sizes.

Two-core flex has no earth core; it's for lights and pendants with no metal parts or double-insulated appliances. Common sizes are 0.5mm² and 0.75mm².

Light bulbs and tubes

Filament lamps come in clear, obscure (pearl) and in a vast range of colours, in standard 'mushroom' shape or decorative gloves, candles and spirals (also tubes for more intense light). Sizes vary, too. They're connected with a two-pin bayonet cap.

Spotlights and floodlights have an internal silver coating or cap: internally silvered (ISL) lamps are silvered round the base and sides to produce a broad beam; crown-silvered (CS) versions have silvered caps to produce a narrow beam and control glare; parabolic aluminized reflector (PAR) lamps have armoured glass for outside use.

Small, decorative and larger specialized lamps sometimes have a threaded Edison Screw (ES) cap as used in Europe.

Fluorescent tubes are normally made in 25 or 38mm (1 or 1½in) diameter and in lengths up to 2.4m (8ft), although miniature versions are made. Wattage is according to tubelength: 10W per 300mm (12in) is a rough guide.

The end fittings are bi-pin caps, which locate into a fitting which contains the wiring and a starter. The tube may be covered by a diffuser or boosted by reflectors.

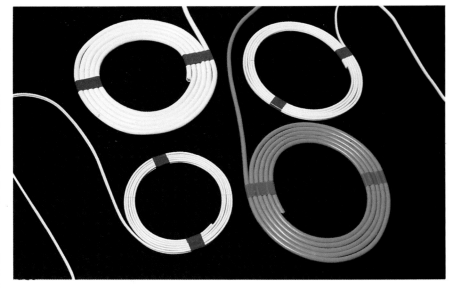

Cable is the fixed wiring for lights and sockets usually hidden under the floorboards or the plaster. Cable is flat in section and grey or white in colour. Flex is for movable appliances.

There is a vast selection of lamps — to suit different purposes — from standard tungsten filament bulbs to striplights, fluorescents, coloured and silvered lamps and a range of decorative candle and pygmy types

Tools

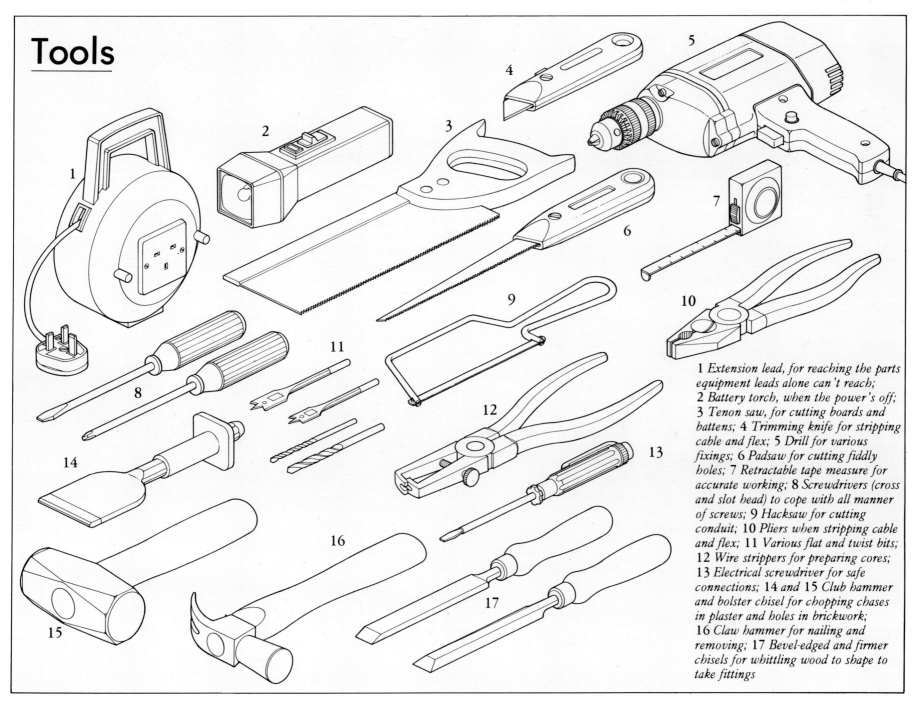

1 Extension lead, for reaching the parts equipment leads alone can't reach; 2 Battery torch, when the power's off; 3 Tenon saw, for cutting boards and battens; 4 Trimming knife for stripping cable and flex; 5 Drill for various fixings; 6 Padsaw for cutting fiddly holes; 7 Retractable tape measure for accurate working; 8 Screwdrivers (cross and slot head) to cope with all manner of screws; 9 Hacksaw for cutting conduit; 10 Pliers when stripping cable and flex; 11 Various flat and twist bits; 12 Wire strippers for preparing cores; 13 Electrical screwdriver for safe connections; 14 and 15 Club hammer and bolster chisel for chopping chases in plaster and holes in brickwork; 16 Claw hammer for nailing and removing; 17 Bevel-edged and firmer chisels for whittling wood to shape to take fittings

CHAPTER 3
Simple lighting jobs

It's not necessary to completely revamp your electrical installation to improve your lighting — there are numerous quick and simple ways to alter the existing set-up, whether it's just a matter of re-arranging the positions of table and standard lamps, according to the suggestions given in the first chapter of this book, or whether you need to add extra fittings or alter the positions of fixed accessories such as the ceiling pendant lights (see page 31). Armed with no more than a screwdriver you will be able to transform your existing scheme by fitting a dimmer switch (see page 29). If you consider that there aren't enough sockets to cope with your arrangement of portable lights, why not swap single ones for doubles — or even add more to the original circuit? Whatever work you do on your electrical system, be sure you know exactly what you're doing, and follow the instructions given exactly. Before you attempt any work, turn off the main isolating switch on the consumer unit and don't turn it back on until you've finished — it's a sensible idea to place a notice on the switch warning anyone why the supply is off. If you're working on a single circuit only, it's enough to remove the appropriate circuit fuse or switch off the MCB, before restoring the supply to the other circuits — keep the fuse with you until you need to replace it. Double-check all the connections that you make. If you are at all unsure, it's best to play safe and call in a qualified electrician.

Fitting a plug

Most small domestic electrical items are supplied without a plug, even though there is a welcome trend for manufacturers to mould a plug on to the lead of the more expensive appliances.

So when you buy a new light, the first thing to do is to check if the lead is long enough for you to use the light in the way that you intend. If it is not, check the thickness of the original wire and fit a suitable length of flex in its place.

Plugs come in two halves, held together with a metal screw. Undo the screw, pull the top off the plug and identify the way in which the wires fit on to the top of the metal pins, and the way the wire is clamped to the body of the plug. Loosen the terminal and clamp screws.

Terminal types
There are basically three types of terminal connection — pillars, where a washer and nut or screw secures the looped flex cores to a screw; stud, where tiny screws hold the cores in holes in the pins; spring-loaded, where the cores are held by a clamp. The cartridge fuse is

Sleeved pins
Due to the risk of children's small fingers finding their way behind a plug that's inserted in a switched-on socket outlet — with potentially tragic results — some manufacturers are producing plugs which have the live and neutral pins half-sleeved in PVC. The ends of the pins are bare as normal, and make connection when inserted in the socket, but if the plug should be pulled half-way out, there is no danger of receiving a shock.

clamped over the live terminal — 13A fuse for powerful appliances rated over 700W; 3A fuse for the rest.

Securing the flex
The flex is secured in a cord grip to

Flex pushed between a jaw-style cord grip cannot be tugged out easily

prevent the cores from pulling out of the terminals. There are various types, the commonest is a fibre strip clamped over the flex, with screws, although the alternative jaw-style grips made in nylon save you having to fiddle with loosening and tightening the tiny screws. Where the flex isn't prepared, trim the outer sheathing with a knife, as shown right. To fit the flex, lay it over the open plug and cut the cores so they reach their terminals — blue to neutral, marked N; brown to live, marked L; green/yellow to earth, marked E or ⏚.

If you are dealing with pillar-type terminals, cut the wire about 6mm longer than is necessary to reach the terminals so that you can wrap the wire round.

Strip off about 10mm of the plastic covering using either wire strippers or a slim pair of pliers. Twist the bare strands of copper together and fit the wire to the terminals.

1. To strip flex, slice carefully down the outer sheathing without knicking the cores inside, then remove excess

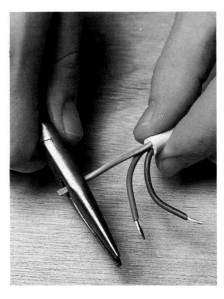

2. Use wirestrippers or pliers to bare about 10mm (³⁄₈in) of the copper conductors, then twist the strands

A correctly wired plug should not have any of the copper cores exposed: the cores shouldn't be under any strain and must be held securely within the terminals. The fuse fits in its carrier over the live (brown) core

Installing a dimmer switch

It's useful to be able to vary the level of illumination in your home to suit your mood and the occasion. A dimmer switch allows you to centralize your options — easy to install, it can reduce electricity consumption and save you money in the long run.

The same level of light doesn't suit all activities and occasions in the home: you need the ability to adjust it from subtle and moody for intimate dinner parties and lolling around in front of the TV, to bright and practical for writing, reading and other specific tasks.

While you can provide all these different requirements with separate lights, dimmer switches offer the versatility to change the mood from a central point. Inexpensive, popular dimmer switches are available as replacements for ordinary on/off switches (table lamp versions are also made) and can be installed in a short time. Dimmers consume less electricity when adjusted from full brilliance, so you can cut fuel bills, if only minimally.

The commonest type is a simple knob mounted on a square plastic faceplate — pressing the knob switches the light on and off; turning it alters the light level. Other dimmers have a separate on/off rocker switch, and there are 'period-style' versions with brass faceplate and knob or modern types with a large dial. You can also obtain two-way dimmers, which are useful in halls and on landings.

Where one switchplate controls two or three lights, you should be able to connect these to a dimmer, so long as you don't exceed the device's total wattage rating and can physically fit the cores into the terminals. If you'd prefer separate switching fit a two-gang dimmer, which

has two control knobs on one faceplate; units with more knobs are also made, but you'd need to fit a larger mounting box for it and they are confusing to use.

More sophisticated dimmers offer automatic operation according to the ambient light level and touch-sensitive — even remote — control.

So far as fitting restrictions go, check that the depth of your present switch mounting box is deep enough for your choice of dimmer; some are slimline, others decidedly chunky: switch off at the mains, unscrew the switch faceplate and pull it forward so that you can insert a tape measure. Unscrew the old box, cut back the brickwork and fit a deeper box if necessary.

2. Connect up the cable cores to the new dimmer switch, according to the manufacturer's instructions

3. Screw the faceplate onto the mounting box, restore the power and test the dimmer switch

1. After switching off at the mains, unscrew the on/off switch faceplate, draw forward and release the cores

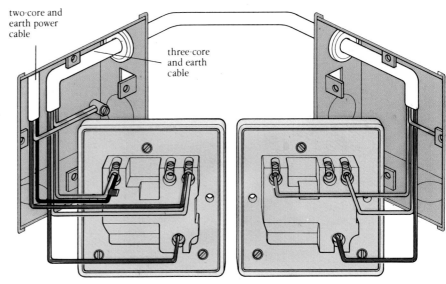

two-core and earth power cable

three-core and earth cable

Two-way switching of dimmers is possible — between downstairs hall and landing, for instance — using special

three-core and earth cable between switches, with power emanating from a standard wall switch position

Automatic cupboard light

Deep, dark cupboards tend to swallow their contents and — unless you resort to a torchlight search — items can go missing indefinitely. Install a miniature light and everything will reappear: fit an automatic switch and you will bless it every time you open the cupboard door.

Depending on the effect you want to give, you can choose either a pigmy filament lamp, a standard light bulb (for a larder-type walk-in cupboard), or a small striplight or fluorescent tube. Filament lamps are cheapest but can cast harsh shadows; fluorescents are more costly but more even in the light they cast. And you need a tube rated only about one quarter of the wattage of a striplight to emit roughly the same level of illumination. Another advantage is that they don't heat up whereas striplights do — this could discolour melamine or veneer.

Size of lamp depends on the area of the cupboard, but generally a 15W striplight is adequate for a standard kitchen unit; 25W lamps are suitable for larger areas.

Door-operated switching
Devices called 'push-to-break' switches are employed in automatic switching — a spring-loaded plunger mechanism is held depressed by the cupboard door, breaking the circuit and so turning off the light; when the door is opened, the plunger springs out, remaking the circuit, and turning on the light. Fittings are available which combine switch and light, although they're more noticeable.

Obtaining power
Although you can obtain power for the cupboard light by teeing into the lighting circuit, it's far simpler to plug it into a socket outlet: fit a three-pin plug (with a 3A fuse) to a length of 0.5mm² flex (see pages 24 and 28) — two-core for switches with plastic cases that don't need earthing; three-core for devices with metal casings or baseplates, where earthing is required. Run the flex into the cabinet from the socket.

At the switch position (see right), cut a 'window' in the outer sheathing lengthways, then round its circumference, taking care not to nick the insulation. Cut the brown (live) wire and strip off about 6mm (¼in) insulation from the ends. Twist the strands together and fit them into the terminals. (If the switch requires earthing, connect the green/yellow core; if there's no terminal, connect the earth wire to a fixing screw.)

Fold the sections of flex together and secure in the cord clamp. Run the flex to the light and connect up.

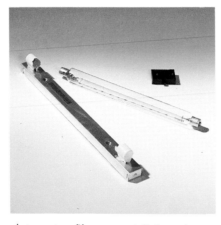

A tungsten filament striplight and an automatic switch for cabinet lighting

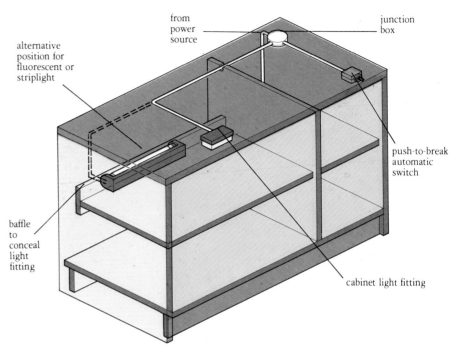

from power source

junction box

alternative position for fluorescent or striplight

push-to-break automatic switch

baffle to conceal light fitting

cabinet light fitting

Screw the push-to-break automatic switch to the carcase where the door will close onto its pushbutton

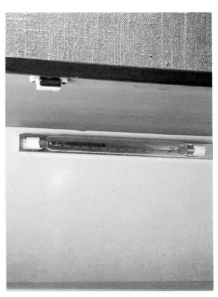

Screw the striplight to the back of the cabinet and run in the wiring as shown in the diagram above

Moving a pendant light

Pendant lights don't always supply the best spread of illumination when suspended from the centre of the room. You can improve the scheme by relocating it over a dining table or seating area.

The way you reposition the pendant depends on whether you have the junction box or loop-in system (see page 22). Turn off the power at the mains and unscrew the ceiling rose cover — if there's one cable, it's the former; if there are two or more, it's the latter.

With the junction box set-up, lift a floorboard in the room above (if you're in a ground floor room) or go into the loft. Cut a 100×19mm (4×¾in) softwood batten to fit between the joists above the old rose and nail it to two 25mm (1in) sq battens nailed to the sides of the joists. Screw a new four terminal junction box to the batten with wood screws.

Disconnect the flex and cable from the old rose and draw the cable into the void. Reconnect the cable cores to the terminals of the junction box, as shown (A). Run in a new length of cable from the new light position to the box and connect its cores (like to like).

With the loop-in system, again disconnect the flex and cables from the rose, draw the latter into the void and reconnect them — with the spur to the new light — to a four terminal junction box fixed to a batten (B).

In either option, refix the rose to the ceiling at the new location. Bore a hole in the ceiling and feed the spur cable through. Strip and prepare the cores — slipping a length of green/yellow PVC sleeving onto the bare earth core. Connect all cores to the rose terminals. Reconnect the flex to the terminals and hook over the hangers for safety.

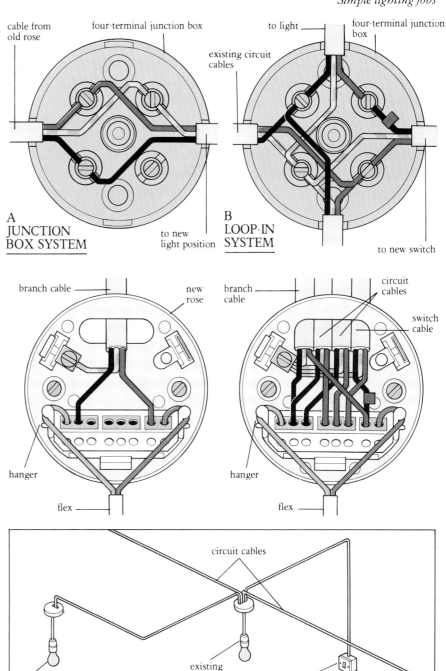

Double up your sockets

A lighting scheme composed of individual table, standard and reading lamps is versatile but it's an arrangement that has a voracious appetite for socket outlets. Don't resort to adaptors — converting single outlets to doubles is the one of the simplest ways to increase your system's capacity.

Don't be tempted to make do with plugs connected to adaptors: not only is this likely to overload the socket's capacity but trailing flexes are also a trip hazard and can overheat if run under carpets and rugs.

So long as your house isn't wired with old rubber-sheathed or lead cables (which are likely to be in dangerous condition and must never be re-wired in this way), there's no reason why you cannot convert all your single socket outlets to double ones.

There are various ways to make the conversion, depending on whether you have flush- or surface-mounted sockets, and whether you want the replacements to look the same. Socket outlets — surface-or flush-mounted — are typically 35mm (1⅜in) deep, although shallower versions only 25mm (1in) deep are made for use with deep faceplates for single-brick and cavity walls, where chopping a recess for flush fixing would mean piercing right through the wall.

Making good connections

Whatever the method you decide to go for, there are two points that you must watch when making the connections:
● If the socket has two or three cables running into it, it's usual to twist together the cores with the same colour coding so they'll be firmly held in the terminals. You cannot do this with your fingers because the copper cores are too stiff; instead, use pliers.
● The PVC insulation on the cores shouldn't allow more than 12mm (½in) of copper core to be exposed: trim it back if the insulation is too short; trim the insulation if that's too long.

Surface single to surface double

The simplest conversion is to replace an existing single surface-mounted socket with a new double surface-mounted box. Unscrew the faceplate of the old box and pull it forward. Release the cable cores from the screw-down terminals. Unscrew the mounting box from the wall and pull it out of the hole.

Take the double replacement box and punch out one of the 'knockouts' in its base to admit the cable: these weak areas in the plastic box can be pressed out easily using the blade of a screwdriver, but you should nibble off any rough edges with a pair of pliers to prevent chafing the cable over the years.

Thread the cables through the hole and press the box against the wall. Mark the wall through its fixing holes, remove the box and drill and plug the wall. Replace the box and secure with countersunk woodscrews driven into the wallplugs. Reconnect the cable cores to the relevant terminals on the new faceplate: red (live) to L; black (neutral) to N; green/yellow striped (earth) to E. The earth core may not have any sleeving: cut a short length of striped PVC to fit and slip it on before making the connection.

Fold the cores up into the box neatly — without any sharp kinks — and press the faceplate against its mounting box. Insert the box screws and tighten them.

Flush single to surface double

Where the existing single socket is flush-mounted, the easiest conversion is to remove its faceplate and fit a new double surface-mounted box on top.

Unscrew the faceplate and release the cable cores. Remove a knockout from the base of the replacement double box and thread in the cables. Align the fixing holes of the new box with the faceplate-fixing lugs of the old box, insert the fixing screws from the old faceplate so that they will match and screw the box in place. Connect the cable cores and screw on the faceplate.

Flush single to flush double

You might consider surface-mounted socket outlets too bulky and opt for flush fixing. This is quite straight-forward, but it can make quite a mess.

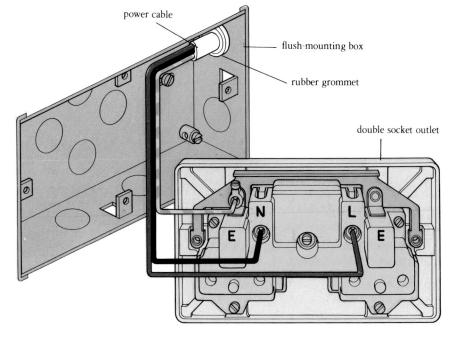

power cable
flush-mounting box
rubber grommet
double socket outlet

Above: *The terminal connections to a double socket outlet are labelled*

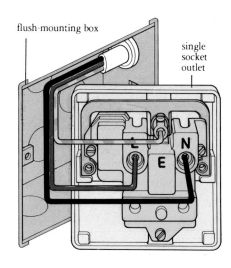

flush-mounting box
single socket outlet

Above: *Similarly, the connections to a single outlet are clearly indicated*

Remove the old single faceplate and mounting box then use the new box as a template for marking its position in pencil on the wall, over the existing hole. Place sheets of newspaper on the floor directly below the socket then chop a line around the box position using a club hammer and bolster chisel. Hack out the plaster or the brickwork to the same depth as the original recess.

Offer up the new box: if it still stands proud of the wall surface, chop away a little more masonry; if it's set too low, trowel a dab of filler onto the back of the recess to bring the box forward sufficiently. Mark the screw fixing positions on the back of the recess, check that they are level, then drill for and insert wallplugs.

Press out a pre-cut knockout from the base or lower edge of the replacement metal mounting box, then slip on a rubber grommet to protect the cables from chafing. Insert the cables through the grommet then position and screw the box to the recess. Make good any gaps around the box with filler then connect the cable cores and screw the faceplate to the mounting box.

Fixing in a hollow wall

Socket outlets are fixed to a hollow stud partition wall either by screwing their surface-mounted boxes to a stud, or to the cladding using spring toggles. Flush boxes are notched into a stud or set within the thin plasterboard cladding, held with flanges or using a cavity wall mounting box.

Converting surface-mounting boxes is easy: simply remove the old box and fit the new one. To fit a new double flush box, use the new mounting box as a template to mark its position on the wall, then cut the hole larger using a padsaw. Screw the box to the notch cut in the stud; if there's no stud, use a cavity wall box, which has integral flanges.

Remove the faceplate of the old single surface-mounted socket and unscrew the mounting box

Simply screw the new double socket's surface-mounting box into new wallplugs over the existing cable exit

Unscrew the faceplate of an old flush-mounted single socket; access may be tight if the cable's short

Punch knockouts from a double surface-mounting box and screw to the single box's faceplate lugs

To replace a flush single with a flush double socket, drill and chisel out a larger recess for the box

Screw the new double flush-mounting box into the enlarged recess, feed in the cable and screw on the box

CHAPTER 4
Improving your lighting

A house can soon outgrow its electrical system as a child outgrows its clothes — and as you purchase more labour-saving devices, you're making increasing demands on the original specification, which might have been basic in the extreme. But there's no reason why you can't rejig the set-up to suit your needs, perhaps by increasing the number of socket outlets and lighting points (see pages 36 to 39) rather than simply altering their positions. Depending on the room you're trying to light, you can install fittings that are more practical or more decorative (see pages 40 and 41), and add controls that make it more convenient or safe for you to use — such as the versatility of two-way switching. And remember the necessity of pull-cord switches in a bathroom, where the mix of water and electricity could be fatal. The following projects tell you how you can make more sense of your lighting system — without resorting to a rewire.

Extending the lighting circuit

A single pendant light dangling from the ceiling in the centre of a large room won't contribute much to your lighting scheme — and it's a simple enough matter to move it, as previously described — but used in conjunction with other fittings, perhaps located at the perimeter of the room and independently switched, you'll have the chance to highlight particular areas and improve the overall illumination.

To install a new ceiling light, it's necessary to connect into a nearby lighting circuit cable, in effect tapping the power. There are basically two ways you can do this, depending on whether your house is wired with the junction box or loop-in system (see page 22). But before you can start, you will have to find out if your circuit can cope with the extra demands the new light or lights will place on it.

Calculate capacity
It's permissible for a lighting circuit to contain up to twelve 100W lighting points, but in practice you should limit this to only eight — this allows you to use lamps of a higher wattage. To discover if your circuits have sufficient capacity, first switch off the relevant MCB or remove the fuse carrier for the circuit in question at the consumer unit.

Now work your way round the rooms turning lights on: note down how many bulbs do not come on and how many watts they add up to. If the result is less than eight lights or the total wattage is less than about 1000W, then it's alright to extend the circuit.

If you discover during your investiga-tions that the circuits are wired in two-core PVC-sheathed cable, which has no earth, you'll have to install a single earth core running from the new light position to the earth terminal on the consumer unit, if you intend to use a fitting with metal parts.

Junction box connection
Whether you have junction box or loop-in wiring, you can extend the lighting by cutting the power cable and inserting a four terminal junction box. From here you take one cable to the new light position and another to a switch to control it (see page 42) at a convenient point.

You can do this by running in the cables to the new rose and switch, clipping them to the sides of the joists (in the loft space or beneath an upstairs floor). Nail a batten between the joists directly below the circuit cable you want to tee into. Screw a four terminal junction box to the batten, cut the circuit cable and strip its cores. Connect the cores to the junction box, sleeving the earth core as usual.

Prepare the cores of the new cables and connect them to the junction box (A). Wrap a flag of red adhesive PVC tape around the switch cable's black core to indicate that this is the switch return, and therefore live when the switch is on.

Loop-in connections
With the loop-in system, you can fit the new spur cable direct to the terminals of a rose, provided that there is sufficient space: you can usually physically insert a maximum of four. Unscrew the rose cover and feed the new cable through into the ceiling space from below.

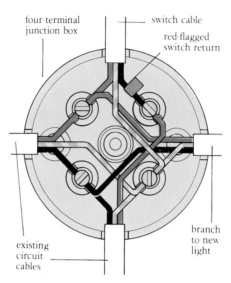

With junction box or loop-in wiring insert a junction box in the power cable, adding light and switch cables

1. *Nail a batten between the joists directly below the power cable you're going to connect into*

2. *With the power switched off, cut the power cable, prepare its cores and reconnect them to the junction box*

3. *Run a branch cable from the new light position and a switch cable, flagging the switch return in red tape*

Strip the outer sheathing and core insulation, then connect them to the live, neutral and earth terminals of the rose (B) — you might have to release the screws that hold the rose to the ceiling to give you enough room.

Run the cable to the new lighting point, clipping it to the sides of the joists. If you want to switch the new light independently, run in another cable from the new ceiling rose to a new wall switch either recessed or on the surface.

Connecting the new light

With both set-ups, connecting the new light is straightforward. Bore a hole in the ceiling at the point you want the fitting to be — it should be fixed to a batten nailed between joists or screwed directly to a joist — and feed the cable through. Fix the new rose to the ceiling with wood screws, prepare the cable cores and connect them to the terminals.

With loop-in wiring you can connect a new spur cable directly to the terminals of the ceiling rose, provided that there is sufficient room

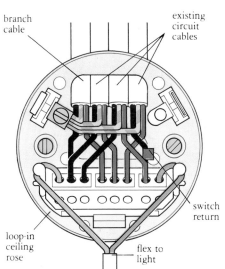

branch cable

existing circuit cables

loop-in ceiling rose

switch return

flex to light

1. *At a loop-in rose, remove the rose cover then feed the new spur cable in through the knockout*

2. *Strip and prepare the live and neutral cores of the spur cable then sleeve the earth in green/yellow PVC*

3. *Connect up the cores of the spur to the relevant terminals of the loop-in rose using pliers to hold them in place*

4. *With loop-in or junction box wiring run the spur cable to the new lighting point, clipping to the sides of joists*

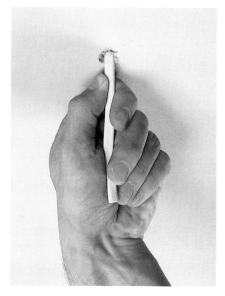

5. *Bore a hole in the ceiling at the new light position and pull the spur cable through and prepare its cores*

6. *Fix the new pendant rose to the ceiling (to a joist or batten between joists) and connect up the cores*

Fitting a close-mounted light

In bathrooms, where there's likely to be a lot of steam, an enclosed close-fitting light is a must for safety's sake — but there are also decorative versions suitable for use in the living room.

Enclosed light fittings are usually available with a plain bowl or globe, which sits flush with the ceiling surface, attached to a special mounting baseplate.

Although straightforward to install with junction box wiring — simply fix the baseplate to the ceiling and connect the cable to the terminal block in the fitting — if you have loop-in wiring, there's no facility to accommodate all the cables so install a junction box above the ceiling and run a cable to the light.

Attaching the baseplate

Although models vary, they're all fitted in a similar way. First switch off the power at the mains and inspect the ceiling rose connections by removing the cover: if you have junction box wiring, remove the old rose.

With loop-in wiring, remove the rose and draw the cables up into the ceiling void. Reconnect all the cores to a four terminal junction box screwed to the side of a joist above the lighting point. Feed a cable through the hole and connect up.

Some bowl fittings have a fixing bar, which must be screwed to the ceiling and the baseplate attached to it, once the connections to the integral terminal block have been made; other fittings simply require the baseplate to be screwed to the ceiling.

Feed the cable into the fitting and slip heat-resistant sleeving over the live and neutral cores.

Left: *The circuit connections for a close-mounted bowl light fitting are similar to those for a pendant fitting*

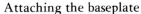

four-terminal junction box

existing power cables

to wall switch

bowl light

switch mounting box

switch faceplate

1. *Screw the bowl light's metal baseplate to the ceiling and pull the power cable through the entry hole*

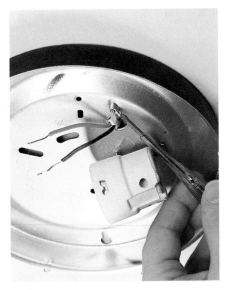

2. *Sleeve the earth core in green/yellow PVC tape and secure to the screw-down baseplate terminal*

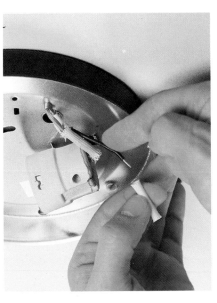

3. *Because the connections are enclosed, it's wise to slip heat-resistant sleeving over the cores*

4. *Connect the cores to the lampholder terminals, fit the bulb then secure the bowl shade to the baseplate*

Fitting a fluorescent light

Fluorescent lights produce glare-free illumination without casting harsh shadows, so they're ideally suited to areas in the home where overall practical lighting is needed, such as the kitchen, bathroom and work-room. But don't dismiss them as being clinical — fluorescents are also able to produce dramatic, stylish effects in living rooms, dining rooms and bedrooms with the aid of baffles and diffusers fitted over the top.

Shapes and sizes

There's a wide range of sizes of fluorescent lights: the larger ones can be used as main room lighting, when fitted with a corrugated or dimpled diffuser to help spread the light. Smaller ones are suitable for concealed lighting behind pelmets to enhance a curtain, or under shelving in alcoves.

Although straight, 'linear' tubes are the most common, circular versions are also worth considering, as they can be equipped with a dainty glass diffuser where appearance counts.

Cheaper to run

Although fluorescent tubes are more costly than ordinary tungsten filament types to install, they're more efficient, cheaper to run, and longer-lived: they last over 5000 hours, about five years' average use. A 1500mm (5ft) tube with a 65W rating emits four times as much light as a 100W light bulb.

The fitting comprises two parts, the lamp and the control gear, usually contained in a metal box or baseplate, which supports a lampholder at each end. The gear includes a starter and a choke to

activate the lamp when it's switched on and control it during use.

Fixing the baseplate

Rigging up a fluorescent light is much the same as installing any close-mounted ceiling fitting, as described on the facing page — if you have junction box wiring, simply remove the old rose and connect the single cable directly to the terminal block on the fitting's baseplate; with loop-in wiring it's necessary to reconnect the cables to a four terminal junction box.

To fit the baseplate, first remove the diffuser and tube and release the cover by removing its retaining screws. Hold the baseplate (or the template, if one was supplied with the fitting) against the ceiling and then mark the ceiling through the screwholes in the baseplate. Check that the screws are going to hit a ceiling joist or fix a batten to take them.

Making connections

Feed in the cable then screw the baseplate to the ceiling. Connect the prepared cores of the cable to the terminal block inside the baseplate, sleeving the earth core with green/yellow PVC if it was previously bare. Where the cable is two-core, run a separate length of 1.5mm² green/yellow PVC-insulated cable from the fitting back to the earth terminal block in the consumer unit.

Replace the cover of the backplate — this may also be retained by spring clips — and insert the tube in its holders, which usually spring outwards for ease of fitting (most tubes use the bi-pin connection). Insert the starter in the socket at the side of the baseplate by twisting it clockwise to secure it.

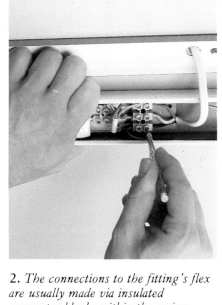

1. Screw the fluorescent light's baseplate to the ceiling and feed the power cable through

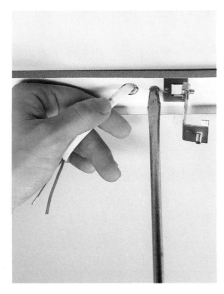

2. The connections to the fitting's flex are usually made via insulated connector blocks within the casing

3. Fit the casing to the baseplate according to the maker's instructions then push the starter into its socket

4. Fit the fluorescent tube in its holders — depending on pin configuration — then snap on diffuser

Lights for a wall

Wall lights allow you to vary the level of illumination in the room, providing either localized lighting for reading, or general mood lighting. Fitted with separate — or integral — switches, they offer adaptable lighting options.

Wall lights often have the edge on table and standard versions because they don't hog floor space, useful table surfaces or power sockets.

Although mounted on the wall, the fittings are easy to connect to the supply using the loop-in or junction box options, as for close-fitting ceiling lights (see pages 38 and 39). Installation in a solid wall calls for cutting a channel (chase) in the plaster surface, so be prepared for some redecorating. In a hollow stud wall you may have to cut the cladding at horizontal noggins to feed the cable down to the light. It is not so neat but you can go for surface fixing using plastic mini-trunking to conceal the cable.

Chop a groove down the wall about 25mm (1in) deep using a club hammer and cold chisel (the light should be positioned about two-thirds the way up the wall) and cut plastic conduit to fit. Wedge it with masonry pins, slot in the cable then make good with plaster. Some wall lights include their own switch (the diagram below shows switching independent of other lights). If the fitting doesn't have terminal blocks at the back, the connections between cable and flex must be made in a non-combustible enclosure such as a terminal conduit (BESA) box — screw the light directly to the box. A slim architrave box can be used for a fitting with a narrow baseplate. Make the connections with a connector block.

Some wall lights have narrow baseplates and a slim flush-mounted architrave box is necessary for making the connections within the wall

1. Mark the screw fixing positions on the wall through the wall light itself, having fed in the cable

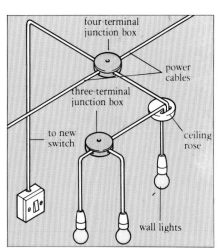

For greatest versatility, your wall lights should be switched independently of the other fittings on the circuit: the wiring

details above show how this can be done with either the loop-in or junction box set-ups

2. Connect up the cable cores to the flex cores via insulated connector blocks then fit the cover

The BESA box is a non-combustible enclosure for connections where there are no terminal blocks at the back

Fitting switches

Switches enable you to control your lights, so it's obvious that they should be placed for convenient use. The basic switch is wall-mounted, but for rooms such as the bathroom, where water is in close proximity, it's necessary to fit ceiling-mounted pull-cord types for safety.

Wall-mounted switches may be flush- or surface-mounted and the most popular type is the plateswitch, which comprises a flat, square faceplate with one or more rocker switches in the centre. There are one-, two- and three-gang units measuring 85mm (3⅜in) square for controlling separate light fittings from one unit; four- and six-gang versions measure 146×85mm (5⅞×3⅜in). Two-way switches are also made (see page 42). Plateswitches are fixed to metal mounting boxes 16 or 25mm (⅝ or 1in) deep. Plaster-depth boxes — the thinner type — are fitted flush with the wall surface and only the thickness of the plaster needs to be cut away.

In a solid wall, just chop a chase from ceiling level to about 1.2m (4ft) above floor level and run in the cable from the ceiling void in conduit. Use the mounting box to mark the position of the switch on the wall, then use a club hammer and bolster chisel to chop out a recess to take it. Remove a knockout from the top edge of the box, fit a grommet, then screw through the back of the box.

Slot the switch cable through into the box and strip its cores carefully. Sleeve the earth core with green/yellow PVC and connect it to the earth terminal on the box itself (on metal faceplates there's usually an earth terminal on the switch itself). The black neutral core serves as the switch return in this instance, so you must wrap a flag of red PVC adhesive tape around it to indicate that it's live.

Insert the red and black cores into the relevant terminals — these are marked L1 (the red core) and L2 (the black core).

Installing a pull-cord switch

A pull-cord switch is fixed in place by screwing the backing plate to a joist or batten between joists, then feeding the cable through for connection to the switch terminals: red to live, black to neutral, green/yellow sleeved to earth. You then simply screw the housing to the backing plate (with some types the backing plate and terminal housing are one unit, and a screw-on cover, slotted onto the pull-cord, fits on top).

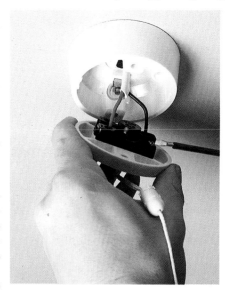

Above: *A pull-cord switch is used in bathrooms, where the proximity of water is a potential shock risk*

Surface-mounted switch. Used where it is difficult or messy to cut through walls

Flush mounted switch. The backing box needs to be fitted into a recess cut in the wall

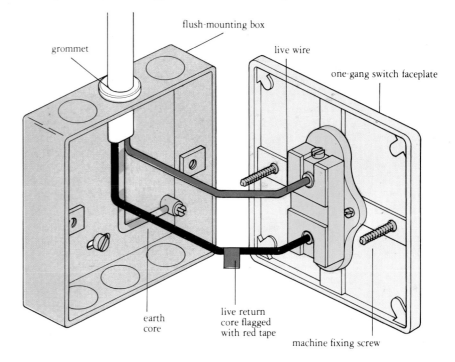

grommet

flush-mounting box

live wire

one-gang switch faceplate

earth core

live return core flagged with red tape

machine fixing screw

Two-way switching

One switch for one light is fine for most rooms, but in some cases — where there's more than one door, or between downstairs hall and upstairs landing, for instance — dual controls are preferable for safety and convenience. Two-way switching provides the solution. At the outset it may look bewildering, but it's quite straightforward if you understand the theory from the start.

A switch at the bottom of a flight of stairs is fine, but what happens when you want to descend and the light's off? This is where a two-way set-up — a switch at top and bottom — excels. In a long hallway, it provides the same convenience but it's also a boon to be able to control the bedroom light from near the door as well as the bedside.

Two-way switching basics

In ordinary one-way lighting, there are two terminals and the switch completes or breaks the electrical connection between them; but in a two-way set-up — you need a two-way switch at both switch positions — there are three terminals. The live supply is connected to the terminal marked C (common) of one switch; terminal C of the other switch is connected to the light that is being controlled.

The terminals marked L1 and L2 are linked in pairs by 'strapping' wires (these are arranged as L1 to L1; L2 to L2). This enables a single light to be controlled from each switch, whatever position the other switch is in.

How the switches are linked

Special 1.0mm² three-core and earth cable is used for linking the two-way switches; unlike ordinary circuit cable, it's colour-coded red, blue and yellow (plus the standard green/yellow sleeving you have to add for the earth core). Red is used for the common-to-common link (that's at the top of a single-gang two-way switch); yellow for the L1-to-L1 link (on the left of the switch); and blue for the L2-to-L2 link (on the right of the switch).

The 'switch drop' cable carrying the power from a three-terminal junction box in the ceiling void, or a loop-in rose, is taken to the nearest two-way switch; its red (live) core is connected to L1 and its black (switch return, flagged red) core to L2. The earth core of the three-core cable (sleeved) links the earth terminals of the two switches and the earth core of the switch drop cable is likewise linked to the earth terminal in the two-way switch, thus providing earthing continuity throughout the two-way switching circuit. See the diagram on p. 29.

Converting one-way to two-way

If you have one-way switching, convert it to two-way by replacing the existing one-way switch with a two-way type. Run a length of three-core and earth cable to the new switch position and install another two-way switch there. Connect the switch drop to whichever of the switches is the nearest.

Running in the new cables

When routing the cables, chop a chase in the plaster using a club hammer and cold chisel then run the cable in plastic conduit held temporarily with masonry pins. Make good the chase later with plaster or filler.

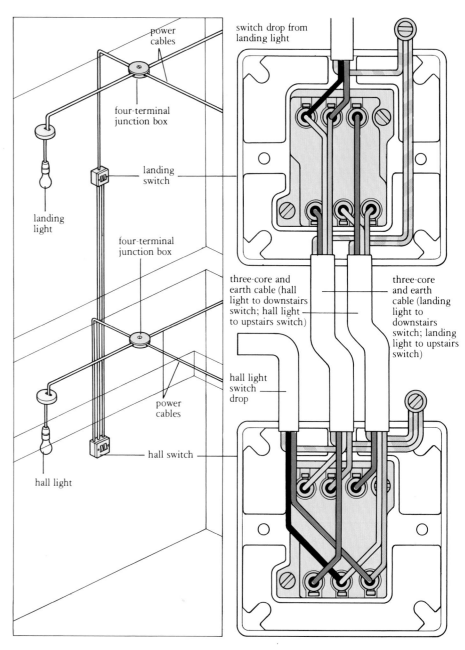

Above: *This arrangement uses two-way switches with two separate controls known as 2-way, 2-gang switches*

Above: *This arrangement for hall and landing allows you to switch each light on and off separately at each switch*

On a hollow stud wall you may be able to drop the cable through the cavity. Drill a hole in the timber plate at the top, in the loft, and drop a weighted length of string down the gap between the two sheets of plasterboard. You might have to cut access holes in the plasterboard cladding where horizontal studs block the weight's progress, then feed the string below to the switch fishing the string out of the hole for the switch with a piece of stiff wire. Tie the cable to the string and pull it through.

If you'd rather not disturb your decor, it's a simple matter to run the switch cable on the surface in plastic mini-trunking, although this can actually detract from the decor you're trying to preserve so carefully.

Switching the hall and landing

To arrange two-way switching at the hall and landing, so that you can switch the landing and hall lights from upstairs or downstairs — not just the landing from the hall and the hall from the hall only — it's necessary to fit two-gang two-way switches, as shown in the diagram.

Take power for the landing light from a junction box or loop-in rose: run a two-core and earth switch drop cable to a new two-gang two-way switch on the landing. From this run a three-core and earth cable which will control the landing light from a switch in the hall downstairs. Run another three-core cable from the upstairs switch to control the hall light.

Downstairs, take power for the hall light from a junction box or loop-in rose and run a two-core and earth switch drop to the second two-gang two-way switch, into which the three-core and earth cables from upstairs have been linked.

Two-way set-up for independent lights

Two-way switching in the bedroom is convenient, saving you having to nip

from between the sheets out into the cold in order to turn the light on or off at the usual doorway position.

If you want two-way control of independently-switched bedside lights, it's usual to employ the services of a special RB4 multi-terminal junction box, which provides a central point for the more complex connections, thus saving on cable in a big way.

Run two-core and earth cable to the RB4 from a three-terminal junction box inserted in the power supply; from there run two lengths of three-core and earth cable to the door switch — a two-gang, two-way type; from the RB4 run two more three-core cables to separate one-gang two-way switches fitted at each side of the bed; two lengths of two-core and earth cable run from the RB4 to the wall lights above the bed complete the circuit.

A three-terminal junction box contains the connections to the power cable

An RB4 multi-terminal junction box centralizes the two-way connections

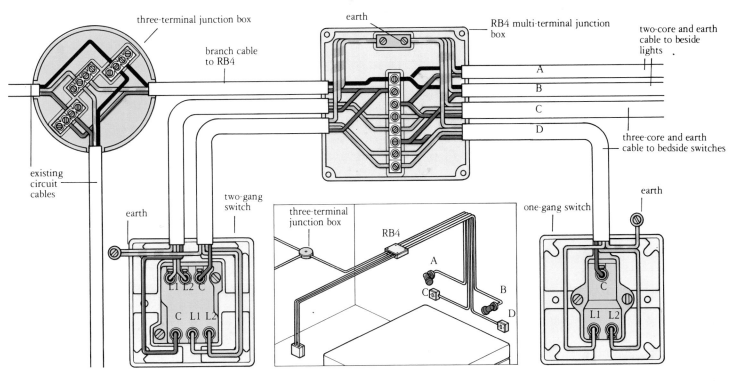

Extending the power circuit

Doubling up on your existing socket outlets is one way to increase your circuit's capacity to accept portable lights, as described previously, but if you want to add sockets where there isn't one to start with, you might be able to expand the circuit to new ground with a simple spur.

It's only feasible to contemplate extending a modern ring circuit — the old style circuits wired in rubber-sheathed cables are likely to be in a potentially dangerous condition anyway.

How to extend the circuit

To extend the ring circuit, it's necessary to add a spur cable, connecting it either into the back of one of the socket outlets or by inserting a 30A three-terminal junction box in the ring cable and adding your branch to that. It's permissible under the Wiring Regulations to add one spur for every socket outlet on the ring.

To your spur you can attach a single socket or a double socket, but not more than one outlet is permitted.

Identifying the ring circuit

Adding the spur isn't complicated — what does present some problems is determining which cables are actually part of the ring circuit, and which are themselves spurs: you aren't allowed to take a spur from a socket that's already on a spur, or tee into a spur cable with a junction box.

To identify which arrangement you have, first turn off the power at the consumer unit, then unscrew the faceplate of the socket outlet where you'd like to add the spur cable. If there is only one cable, this means:

● the socket is at the end of a spur.
  If there are three cables:
● the socket is a ring socket and it has a spur already connected.

You are not allowed to extend either of these sockets. If the socket has two cables, it could either be:
● a ring socket.
● the intermediate socket on an old spur (when two outlets were permitted).
● a socket on an old radial circuit.

Using a continuity tester

To eliminate further the unsuitable set-ups and reveal the ring circuit's identity, either trace the cables around the house or use a continuity tester.

Proprietary continuity testers are made, but there's no need to go to the expense of buying one: it's a simple matter to make one from a 4 volt battery, a length of twin bell wire and a torch bulb and holder. Part the insulated cores of the bell wire at one end and attach the cores to the terminals of the battery. About halfway down the wire, cut one of the cores and connect the stripped end to the torch holder terminals. Part and strip the cores at the other end of the wire.

Switch off the power at the mains and disconnect the two live (red) cable cores connected to the faceplate of the socket in question. Separate the two wires and touch one wire from the tester to each of the circuit wires. If the bulb lights, the socket is on a ring. If it stays off, it's on a spur or a radial.

Where you'd prefer to take your spur from a junction box, use the tester to determine whether the cable is on a ring by cutting through it and touching the leads to the live cores exposed at the ends.

1. *Draw round the mounting box, then use a club hammer and bolster chisel to chop a hole in the masonry to set it flush with the plaster surface*

2. *Screw the mounting box within the recess into wallplugs then run in the new spur cable, connect the cores and attach to the faceplate*

3. *If you don't want to go to the trouble of chopping a recess for a flush-mounted box, simply screw a surface-mounted box to the wall*

4. *In a partition wall, you'll have to cut an access panel and fit a noggin between studs to take the mounting box if positioning is critical*

If the bulb did not light, how can you tell whether or not the socket or cable is a spur or a radial? The only course left open to you is to trace the cables around the house. If it leads directly back to a ring socket and on to a socket that has only one cable, it's a spur. If it leads back to the consumer unit and loops on to more than one socket, it's a radial circuit. You can extend the latter, if the area it serves is less than 20sq m (215sq ft) and it is wired in 2.5mm² cable.

Running in the spur cable

Assuming that you've identified the ring circuit, switch off the power and then unscrew the faceplate of the socket on the ring. Insert the end of a length of 2.5mm² cable, stripped of its outer sheathing and its core insulation cut back by about 10mm (³⁄₈in).

Connect the cores to the relevant terminals, twisting them together with the existing cores. Route the cable to the new socket position — you'll have to lift some floorboards to enable you to feed the cable through, unless you opt for the easier surface fixing in mini-trunking.

If the cable run is parallel to the joists, you shouldn't have much trouble, but if it's at right-angles, drill holes through the joists (about 50mm/ 2in from the top) and feed the cable through.

At the new socket position, use the metal backing box as a template for marking the position, then chop a recess for it in the plaster. Screw the box in place and run in the spur cable. Connect up the cores and screw on the faceplate.

To make the connection from a three terminal junction box, lift a floorboard to find the ring cable then fit a batten between the joists directly under it. Screw the junction box to the batten, cut the power cable and reconnect it to the box terminals, sleeving the earth core. Run in the spur cable.

1. *At the ring circuit socket outlet, remove the faceplate and run in the spur cable from the new socket*

2. *Clip the spur cable to the sides of the joists, passing it through the timbers if it runs parallel to them*

3. *At the new socket, prepare the cable cores, sleeve the earth core and connect to the new double socket*

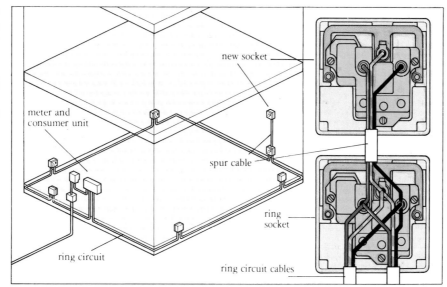
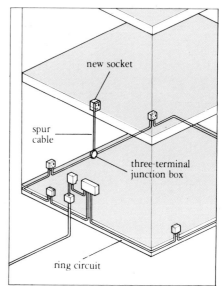

In a ring circuit arrangement, the simplest way to provide an extra socket outlet is to connect into the back of a

ring socket and run the spur cable to the new socket position, connecting as shown above

Alternatively, where you want to save on long cable runs, insert a junction box in the ring cable and spur from it

CHAPTER 5
Decorative lighting ideas

Switches, sockets, fluorescents, as described in the previous chapter, are used primarily for their practicality in helping to control your lighting schemes but there is a range of fittings and accessories which boast more decorative purposes. Downlighters, wall washers, eyeball spotlights and tracklights, for example (see pages 48 to 51), provide the finishing touches to an efficient, successful lighting arrangement by accentuating certain features in the room — imposing curtains across a window, for instance, or an attractive arched alcove. They create soft pools of illumination or highlight a feature wall with scalloped beams of light, without directly flooding the room with a harsh glare. The more ornate fittings (see pages 52 and 53) can help to retain the charm and character of a period home and at the same time provide the quality and variety of lighting that today most people expect.

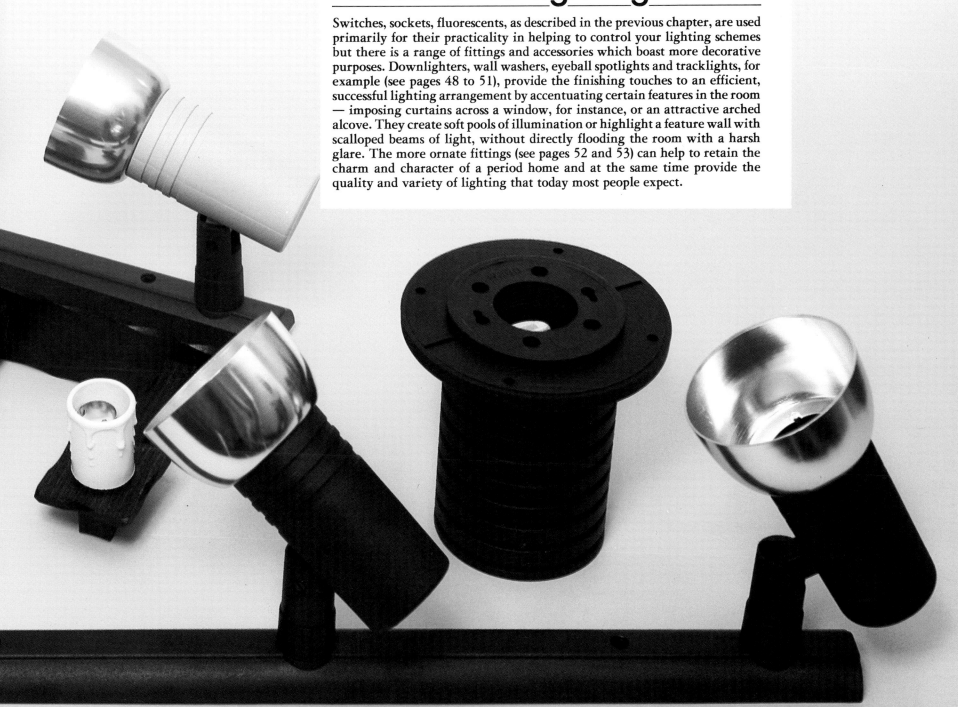

Installing recessed lights

If you consider that it's the light that's more important than the fitting, recessed lighting is for you. This type of fitting stays well out of the way within the ceiling void yet the light it casts is both efficiently functional and decoratively discreet. And where space aloft doesn't permit a totally hidden fitting, there's a range of unobtrusive lights which are bound to fit the bill.

The most popular style of recessed fitting is the downlighter — a tubular casing that's fitted in a hole cut in the ceiling, with its lower edge virtually flush with the surface; some versions of the fitting are only semi-recessed.

The wallwasher is a close relation of

the downlighter: basically a similar fitting, it has a baffle which directs the light at an angle of about 45° to illuminate a wall surface or feature.

A third recessed light is the eyeball spotlight, the head of which can be swivelled through 360° to enable items and surfaces to be highlighted.

Perhaps the ultimate in recessed lighting is the illuminated ceiling, which comprises banks of fluorescent tubes (see page 41) fixed to the original ceiling surface, with a grid framework — typically extruded aluminium strips — in which are slotted sheets of translucent panels. The panels diffuse the light, casting an overall, even light; it's used almost exclusively in kitchens and

bathrooms, although individual translucent panels can be set quite successfully in a living room ceiling.

Most recessed fittings can usually be accommodated within a ground floor ceiling void and certainly in an upstairs one below the roof space. The main requirement is to ensure that the fitting is protected from knocks where it projects above the joists. In any case, check the light dimensions carefully and compare them with the fitting space before you start.

A semi-recessed light may solve the problem, or you can buy a fitting in which the lamp is offset to one side, reducing the overall depth required for installation. Alternatively, it's a simple matter to construct a timber box to fit over the fitting to protect it from harm. Before you buy, however, it's as well to check the depth above the ceiling in question so you can purchase the most suitable fitting.

Power to your lights

Tapping into the mains circuitry to supply your new lights isn't complicated: if the lights are to be located close to the main lighting circuit, simply break into it and install a four terminal junction box. Run a length of 1.0mm² two-core and earth cable to the fitting and another to a switch position.

Where the lights are going to be remote from a lighting circuit, insert a three terminal junction box in the power cable and run a spur to a four terminal junction box near the new lights: from this you can attach a switch feed and return cable, plus two feed cables to a pair of downlighters. The diagram on the left shows a typical circuit arrangement supplying a switch and a single recessed light: note that there's still space in the four terminal junction box to take another cable to feed a second light.

By virtue of their design, it's likely that you'll want to install several recessed lights for an area of lighting — say, the perimeter of the room, or spaced across its area. You can supply power to these lights by looping the mains cable in and out of each fitting, all of which will be controlled by a single switch.

Installing a recessed light

Plot the rough position for your new light and look in the loft space or lift a floorboard in the room above the ceiling in question to check that no joist, plumbing pipework or other obstruction will prevent you from fitting the light. Poke a hole through the ceiling from above using a bradawl.

Installation details vary between different fittings, but they're all basically the same. Set a pair of compasses to the diameter of the fitting — check this with the manufacturer's instructions — then scribe a circle on the ceiling. Drill a hole just inside the circle so you can insert a blade of a padsaw: cut around the guideline and sand off the cut edge.

Pull the mains cable through the hole, prepare its cores then connect them to the special terminal block that's commonly attached to the fitting — red (live) to the terminal with a brown flex core leaving it; black (neutral) to the terminal with a blue flex core. Sleeve the earth core with green/yellow PVC and retain in the earthing terminal. It's wise to use special heat-resistant cable for connection to the light, or simply sleeve the live and neutral cores with heat-resistant insulation.

Insert the fitting in the hole, after removing any detachable trim that's necessary. Adjust the lampholder so the lamp will be at the correct level and secure the spring arms holding it flush with the ceiling. Replace the trim and insert the lamp in its holder.

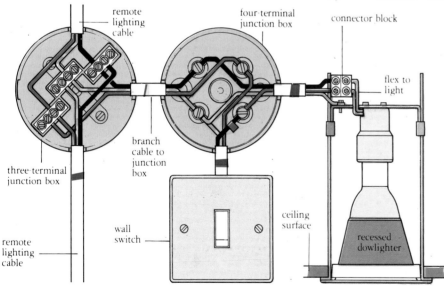

Fit a three-terminal junction box in a lighting cable, run a branch to a four- terminal junction box, another to the switch and one to the light

Protecting the fitting

The recessed downlighter shown in the photographs, right, is slotted into the ceiling to the depth you prefer and retained with a collar, which screws to the ceiling surface. The connections are housed within the tubular casing.

Other fittings require a protective box of timber to be fitted around them if

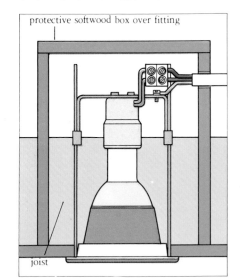

they're located in a vulnerable spot. Cut four panels of 150×25mm (6×1in) softwood or chipboard and nail them together, making a butt-jointed box; fit another panel on one end as a top, then simply place the open-ended box on the ceiling surface.

Heat-resistant pad

Although internally silvered lamps direct most of the heat and light they produce downwards, it's advisable to attach a heat-resistant pad — of mineral fibre ceiling tile, for instance — to the underside of the floorboards above the fitting. The pad can be screwed directly to the floorboards (or the original ceiling if you're installing the lights in a lowered ceiling) using nuts as spacers.

1. *Draw around the recessed light fitting for cutting a hole in the ceiling to take it. Smooth off the edges*

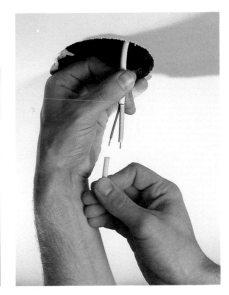

2. *Connect the flex according to the terminal connections then slip heat-resistant sleeving on the cores*

3. *Slot on the light fitting's casing then connect the flex cores to the lampholder terminals*

4. *Push the casing to the depth you want, then secure with the special clip provided with the fitting*

5. *Fit the outer ring over the downlighter casing and screw in place, then fit the lamp in the holder*

Eyeball fittings can be swivelled to illuminate decorative features

Fitting spot & track lights

Versatility in your lighting arrangements — particularly the ability to alter the positions of the fittings — prevents you from becoming bored with the same effects. Spotlights can be swivelled to vary the scheme and when fitted to a track, can be moved across the ceiling for a new accent.

There are numerous types of spotlights, either single fittings or two, three or more lights in a cluster attached to a baseplate or stem, or individual lights which you can fit in a sliding track. All types of light are intended for surface-mounting on the ceiling and the way they're attached and connected to the mains depends on whether there's room behind the baseplate to accommodate the connector block — many types must be fitted to a plastic or metal terminal conduit (BESA) box recessed into the ceiling surface, to both support the weight of the fitting and provide a non-combustible chamber for the connections.

Tapping the power supply

The way you provide power for your spotlights depends on whether you have junction box or loop-in wiring (see page 22). If the former, connection may simply be a matter of removing the old ceiling rose and linking the light fitting's flex to the single two-core and earth cable, using a three-way insulated connector block. With loop-in wiring remove the rose and fit a BESA box.

Fitting a BESA box

A terminal BESA box must be securely fixed to the ceiling, as it usually has to support the weight of the light fitting. First turn off the power at the mains and disconnect the original ceiling rose; pull the cable or cables back above the ceiling.

Hold the BESA box against the ceiling and draw around it. Drill a row of starter holes to admit a padsaw blade, then cut out the circle of plasterboard or lath-and-plaster. The old rose might have been attached to a joist, and in this case you'll have to notch the timber to take the BESA box. Drill into the joist with a large wood bit then neaten the notch with a chisel. Insert the BESA box in the hole — entry slot conveniently positioned to accept the cables — and attach it to the joist with a single woodscrew.

Where the BESA box is being installed between joists, nail a softwood batten between the joists and screw the box to it. With the box installed, insert the circuit cables ready for connection.

Attaching the spotlight

With some spotlights there may be room behind the baseplate for the terminal connectors — particularly if you have junction box wiring, where they'll only be one cable — so no BESA box is necessary: simply connect the cores to the connector block.

A fitting which needs a BESA box is also straightforward to fit. Pull the feed and switch cables into the box and red-flag the black core of the switch return cable. Twist together the lives, neutrals and earths and connect to three separate connector blocks. Connect the taped switch core to a fourth block then push all four into the BESA box.

Offer up the light fitting and connect its flex cores to the blocks — blue to the terminals with the black cable cores; brown to the terminal with the black switch return core; green/yellow to the terminal with the sleeved earth cores. Screw the fitting's baseplate directly to the BESA box's integral screw holes to complete the fixing.

Putting up a tracklight

A tracklight system comprises a length of metal channelling, commonly about 1m (3ft) long, which can be coupled to extend the span. Special spotlights are slotted into the channel and can be slid along to whatever position you prefer. You can fit lamps of the same design, or

A spotlight with no room in its baseplate for connections must be fitted to a terminal BESA box

opt for a mix of different styles — different makes are not usually compatible, however. Some tracks feature fixed-position lights which have adjustable lamp heads.

The cable-to-flex connections are concealed within the track and the leads themselves run in the channel for neatness (although they usually loop out at each fitting to allow the lamp head to be moved freely).

There are basically two ways you can

Spotlights and tracklights complement each other well in a number of guises for versatile lighting. A variation on the standard track light is the cluster, on which individual lights are mounted on a circular baseplate

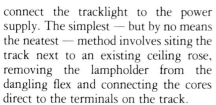

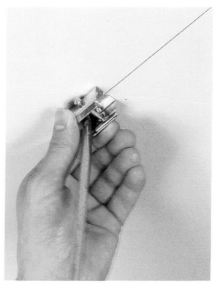

1. *To fit a tracklight, first mark its position on the ceiling then screw a mounting bracket at each end*

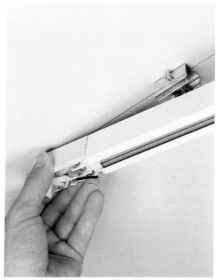

2. *Run the power cable into the track itself, clip the casing on the support brackets and tighten the screws*

3. *Connect up the prepared power cable cores to the screw-down terminal blocks on the track light*

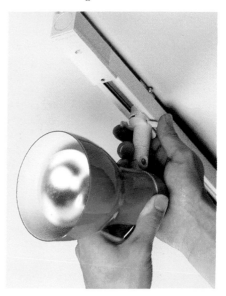

4. *Slot the individual spotlights into the track's channel, secure as instructed, then slide into position*

connect the tracklight to the power supply. The simplest — but by no means the neatest — method involves siting the track next to an existing ceiling rose, removing the lampholder from the dangling flex and connecting the cores direct to the terminals on the track.

Alternatively, remove the rose and

A simple adjustable spotlight

connect the cable to the track: there's no facility for loop-in connections, so you'll have to install a junction box and run a single cable to the track light.

Fitting the track itself is an easy matter of screwing it to the ceiling joists.

A rise & fall light

Lights that slide along a track are a great way to vary your room lighting but a fitting that can be pulled down from the ceiling to the height you prefer is a definite boon to dual-purpose through rooms such as a combined living and dining area, where a light over the table is required only at mealtimes.

Rise-and-fall light fittings are ingenious devices that allow you to pull the lamp head and shade to a level you find most conducive to a particular activity — whether you're dining at the table, working at a desk, or simply that you have low-level seating in a room with a particularly high ceiling.

Numerous styles of rise-and-fall light are made, from the popular globe- or coolie-shaded modern lamp intended for over-dining table installation (and which make a special point of concealing their working parts within a concertina sleeve), to the ornate reproduction models which unashamedly feature complex pulley arrangements and oil-lamp style fittings.

How the unit is attached

Whatever the type, they're basically all fitted in the same way. It's necessary to install a terminal conduit BESA box, as described on the previous pages, both to house the connections from the mains and to provide a firm support and fixing for what can often be a quite weighty accessory at the other end.

Most rise-and-fall devices come with a base plate which incorporates a hook to take the pulley unit. The plate is fitted with machine screws at each end, which are designed to fit into the integral threads of the BESA box.

Connection to the mains is the same as for other ceiling-mounted fittings: that is, by connecting the cables from a loop-in ceiling rose or the single cable from a junction box rose to an insulated connector block, into which the fitting's flex cores are inserted.

Fitting the rise-and-fall unit

With the BESA box installed and the cable cores connected to the terminals of the relevant number of connector blocks, as detailed for fitting spotlights on the previous page, screw the light's hooked baseplate into place.

Hook the rise-and-fall device over the hook and adjust the up and down movement, if necessary, by tightening or loosening the control screw on the side.

Push the plastic cover attached to the concertina sleeve, which conceals the rise-and-fall unit, up to the ceiling and secure it with a grub screw, usually located in the side of the cover.

Chandelier fittings

Modern purpose-made light fittings usually come with their own fixings and terminal blocks, but some decorative lights, conversions from old fittings — typically chandelier styles and heavyweight pendants — are sold without any means of connecting up the cable cores, insufficient space behind their bracket for making them, or a surface fixing bracket that's too small for connection to a terminal conduit box.

If your fitting has a hook and small bracket but no terminal block, make the electrical connections inside a BESA box

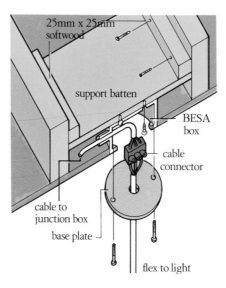

The best way of fixing a BESA box between two joists is to screw it to a support board which bridges the gap

A rise-and-fall unit is the most versatile way to light a table

Most fittings comprise a ceiling-mounted pulley

Some ceiling support units come in two parts: one part has a terminal block, the other a hook for the light

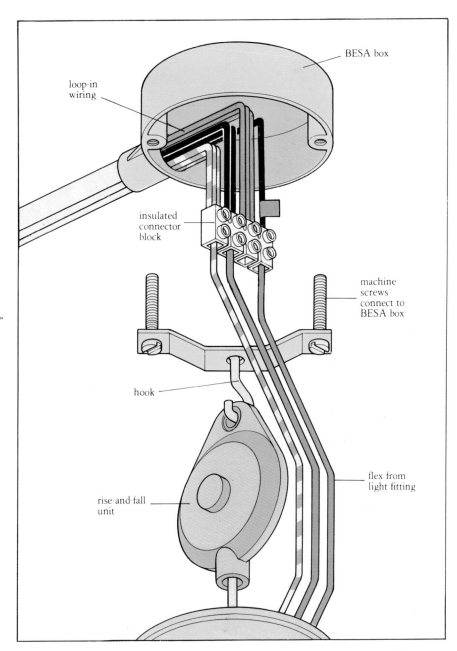

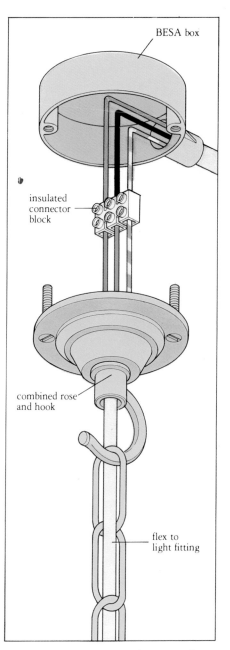

fitted with a cover plate, then screw the bracket and hook to a joist nearby to support the weight of the fitting.

Chain fittings are a typical type of period-style light, which often don't have suitable fixings for modern electrical connections (although some manufacturers produce reproduction versions which have all the necessary fixtures and fittings. One such is a proprietary device — called the Ceiling Master — which comprises two parts: a terminal block to which the cable can be attached; and a hook fitting which contains a second terminal block to take the fitting's flex. To fit the device, the cable and flex are connected as normal, then the hook section is slotted onto the baseplate section and secured: electrical contact is made by three spring-loaded pins meeting three contacts. The chain from the lampholder and shade can then be suspended from the hook.

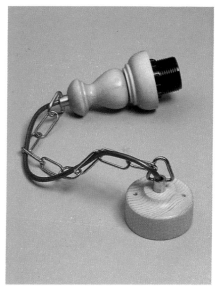

The pulley of the rise-and-fall unit hooks onto a bracket, which must be screwed directly to the holes of a BESA box, in which the connections between the cable and flex are made via insulated connector blocks

A chain-hung chandelier-type fitting which is most suitable for heavy, decorative period-style lights

A chain-hung fitting can be screwed directly to a BESA box. Connections are made via a connector block

CHAPTER 6
Outdoor lighting

Plan for outside lighting in the same way that you provided artifical illumination for the interior of your house: simply from a security point of view, a well-lit house is a deterrent to would-be thieves, who'd understandably much rather plunder a property that offered no signs of life. But protecting your home isn't the only reason why you should install outside lights. For sheer practicality, a porch light (see page 56) is a must, especially if your entrance is shrouded by foliage, not only to ward against prowlers but also to give a cheery greeting to more welcome visitors. And if you have a separate garage or outbuilding, why not include that in your lighting scheme (see page 57) — returning home late at night, you'll appreciate the benefit of a light to see by rather than resorting to a torch; if you need to fetch tools from the shed at night for an emergency repair job, a light at the bottom of the garden will prevent you tramping through the flower beds. If you entertain on summer evenings with barbecue parties, what better way to create the right atmosphere than by stringing up decorative coloured lights?

A light for the porch

A well-lit entrance not only offers a welcome to night-time guests, but also helps prevent accidents on dark nights — and discourages prowlers.

The prime difference between a porch light and a conventional light is that the former should be able to withstand the elements. Take note of the British Standard classification for exterior lights, which spans from: 'drip-proof' for a light in an enclosed porch to 'jet-proof', which can withstand the jet from a hose; for a light mounted outside the porch, go for 'rain-proof', or 'splash-proof'.

Lights are usually sited where they'll cast the best light over the front or back door — commonly on the wall to one side or above the door.

There's a bewildering array of porch lights on the market and you should try to choose one that suits the style of your house. Typical versions include carriage or hanging lanterns (usually plastic or metal with transparent plastic or glass 'windows'), bulkhead fittings (a solid base and a glass cover, with perhaps a wire guard), globes (modern versions of carriage lanterns), brick lights (rectangular, square or circular boxes) or spotlights (using outdoor PAR lamps).

Wiring up the light

Due to the proposed light's proximity to the upstairs floor, it's probably best to take your power from either the existing lighting circuit feeding the downstairs

1. *Mark the position of the porch light's basplate on the exterior wall; run in the supply cable*

2. *Connect up the cable to the light's terminals (inside a BESA box if necessary) then fit the cover*

lights — the most straight-forward method — or from the ring main serving the upstairs socket outlets.

First fit the light to the exterior wall and run the new branch cable back to the cut-in point. Make the hole through the wall to take the feed cable using an electric hammer drill fitted with a 10mm (³⁄₈in) long-reach masonry bit (you can hire these): measure from both sides of the wall, using a common reference point — a window or door — to ensure that when you drill through from one side you won't align with a joist or other obstruction on the other side.

Slot the cable through the hole in a length of plastic conduit then use the base of the light to mark its fixing positions. Mounting and wiring details vary: if it's double insulated, it requires no earth, so cut back the bare core flush with the outer sheathing; if it is earthed, sleeve the core and then connect it securely to the

relevant terminal.

Connect the 1.0mm² two-core and earth cable to the light's flex via an insulated connector block, enclosed within the base — with some bulkhead fittings you simply connect the cable direct to the lampholder.

Screw the fitting to the wall, sealing with mastic if there's no gasket. Run the cable back to the connection point, clipping it to the sides of the joists. Wire up the cable in one of three ways: to a junction box inserted in the existing lighting circuit or to the terminals of a loop-in ceiling rose.

If you take the power from the ring main, use 2.5mm² two-core and earth cable to run a spur from a socket to a switched fused connection unit fitted with a 5A fuse, which allows you to connect the 1.0mm² cable from the light into it. The unit is fixed in exactly the same way as a conventional socket.

Power the porch light by inserting a junction box in the lighting circuit serving the downstairs lights; replace the one-gang switch controlling the hall light with a two-gang version so you can control both lights

Labels in illustration: existing circuit cables; four-terminal junction box; existing hall light; mounting box; two-gang switch

Light to an outbuilding

If your garden shed doubles as a workshop, or you're a budding car mechanic, it's likely that you'll want to continue tinkering after dark. Extend your house's electricity supply via underground or overhead routes to illuminate your hideaway.

With an electrical supply taken outdoors, you'll not only be able to supply light to the garage or workshop but also power, too, for running tools and other equipment. However, special care is needed when running cables outside the house — there's an increased danger of accidental damage to the circuit, by garden spades and hedgetrimmers for instance, and there's more likelihood that sockets, switches and other fittings will get wet; electricity and water are a potentially lethal combination.

Circuit requirements

A power supply to a garage, greenhouse or shed must be provided by a separate radial circuit. The cable for this circuit can run either overhead on taut wires or underground, protected in tough conduit. (Although you can buy special cable for outdoor supplies, it can be awkward to work with, and it is not permissible to use ordinary PVC-sheathed two-core and earth cable.)

If you're installing socket outlets in the outbuilding — say, to power a car inspection lamp — you can use ordinary plastic types, but they're not the best choice for durability and you'd be better off with tough impact-resistant metal-clad fittings for complete safety.

You can take power for the new outdoor circuit either by:
● using a spare 3A fuseway in the consumer unit — if there isn't a spare one, you may be able to buy a new rewirable or cartridge fuse or MCB of the correct rating and install it in the consumer unit, space permitting, in the correct position (highest rating nearest the unit's isolating switch).
● installing a new switchfuse unit (a small consumer unit) near the consumer unit. Get the electricity board to re-route the meter tails — the large red and black cables entering the consumer unit from the meter and board's fuse — to take in the new addition via a 'distribution box' (because only two meter tails can enter the consumer unit); run a separate circuit to the outbuilding starting from the new

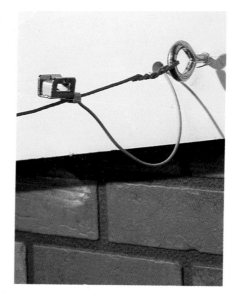

A catenary wire must be earthed by running a copper core, sleeved, from the earthing point to an earth clamp

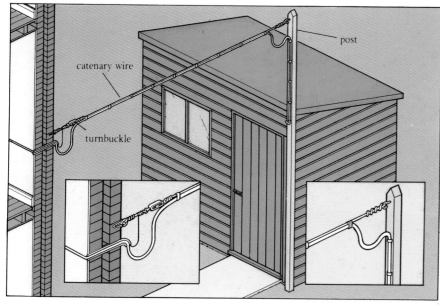

The cable route from the house to an outbuilding can be made overhead by stringing it on catenary wire fixed at least 3.5m (11ft) above the ground

Run the circuit cable through the hole drilled through the wall, allowing an ample loop for rainwater to drip off

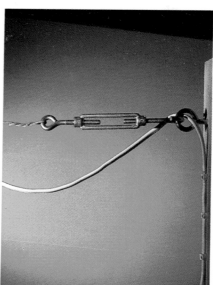

At the outbuilding, stretch the catenary using a turnbuckle. Run in the cable, clipping it to the post

switchfuse unit.

In the outbuilding, the radial circuit cable can be connected to:
● a 30A switched fused connection unit from which you can run socket outlets; power lights by installing a 5A spur from the power cable.
● a new switchfuse unit in the outbuilding, which can supply 5A lighting and 30A power circuits from individual fuses or MCBs.

Extra protection

An ordinary fuse or MCB isn't sufficient protection against the dangers of electric shock in an outside supply, so it's necessary to fit an earth-leakage circuit breaker (ELCB), sometimes called a residual current device (RCD) in the new switchfuse unit to provide better protection against potentially dangerous earth faults — seek the advice of your supplier.

You could ask the electricity board to fit the ELCB in the cable entry to the master consumer unit, for protection of the entire house and outbuilding circuits.

Running an overhead supply

An overhead electrical supply to an outbuilding must be fixed at least 3.5m (11ft) above ground, and 5.2m (17ft) if over a driveway. For a span greater than about 3.5m (11ft) you'll have to support the cable on special catenary wire fitted at the house wall to an eyebolt and at the outbuilding to a securely fixed stout post via a strainer bolt.

Fix the eyebolts at each end of the run first, then stretch the catenary wire between them. Run in a length of 6mm² two-core and earth cable (for a 30A supply) and clip it to the catenary with special cable hangers — you must leave deep loops between each tie so that rainwater won't run along the cable, so allow about 300mm (12in) extra when you cut to length.

It's necessary to earth the catenary wire by running a single green/yellow sleeved core of 6mm² cable from the consumer unit's earthing block to an earth clamp fixed onto the wire.

Running an underground supply

For a buried cable run, dig a trench about 500mm (20in) deep — you can hire a special trench-digging tool to make the job easier — from the cable exit point near the house to the point where it enters the outbuilding. Avoid a route

Rigid PVC conduit comes in various diameters, complete with elbow fittings and straight connectors

Dig the trench, line with sand, then assemble conduit to span the trench and run up the walls at each end

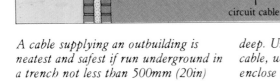

A cable supplying an outbuilding is neatest and safest if run underground in a trench not less than 500mm (20in)

deep. Unless you use special armoured cable, which can be difficult to use, enclose the cable in plastic conduit

Protect the conduit from accidental damage by covering it with a piece of paving slab or ridge roof tiles

Fill in the trench with earth and compact well in. Allow to settle for a few weeks before sowing or paving

that crosses flower beds or vegetable plots, where deep digging could disturb the cable; run it alongside a garden path or wall instead.

Add a layer of sand to the bottom of the trench then run in ordinary 6mm² PVC-sheated two-core and earth cable in rigid PVC conduit: you can buy this in various diameters and lengths, complete with the necessary push-fit elbows and connectors. Thread in the cable first then piece together the conduit, using solvent-weld cement to glue the lengths together. Where the run changes directions, insert elbow fittings of conduit which include screw-on access 'hatches': this is handy when feeding in the cable where it could otherwise become wedged.

Take the conduit up the wall at each end, clipping it in place with special brackets and run it through a hole drilled in the wall. Cover the conduit with sand then place protective ridge tiles or stones over the conduit in the trench. Fill in with top soil up to ground level.

Connections in the outhouse
What you do in the outbuilding depends on the facilities you want: for a few socket outlets and a light, just connect the cores of the radial circuit to a switchfuse unit containing two fuses or MCBs. From here, run 2.5mm² and 1.5mm² cables to and socket outlets and lights respectively, but beware of exceeding the 30A current rating of the radial circuit.

If your radial circuit is simply a branch from a 30A fuseway in the house's consumer unit, feed sockets directly from it, but install a 5A switched fused connection unit in it so that you can run 1.5mm² lighting cable from it.

Connections in the house
In the house, switch off the power at the mains and take the new radial circuit cable to the consumer unit or new

switchfuse unit, clipping it to the baseboard with cable clips.

Strip the cable cores and connect to the relevant terminals, remembering to sleeve the earth core. If you're at all unsure of what to do regarding connection to the mains, seek professional advice — if you're adding a new circuit to the consumer unit, or you require the meter tails re-routing, you **must** call in the electricity board to make the connections and check out the new installation. Be warned, though: the board can refuse to reconnect your supply if they consider that the installation has been endangered by your new addition. This means you should be especially careful when making connections — and don't be tempted to take short cuts.

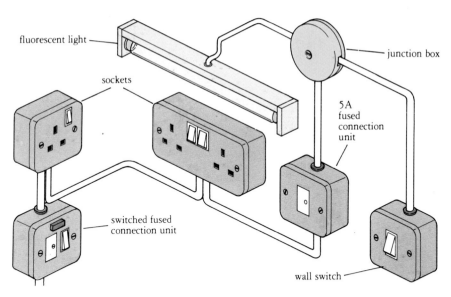

A basic circuit comprising switched fused connection unit from which to run socket outlets and light fitting

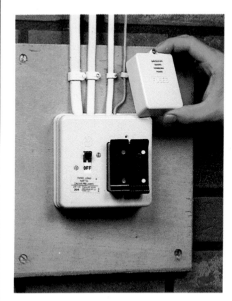

A new switchfuse unit can be used to supply 5A lighting and 30A power circuits from fuses or MCBs

The outdoor circuit can be taken from a spare fuseway of the correct current rating in the consumer unit, using 1.5mm² two-core and earth cable

Low-voltage garden lights

Garden lighting is essential if you plan to hold barbecue parties — it can be functional by illuminating the area and decorative by enhancing splendid specimens of trees or other features in the plot: the fish pond, too, can assume a glowing aura with submerged lights. As a strictly practical addition, path lights and gate lights ensure that a trip down the garden isn't literally that. Low-voltage kits make the job simple and remove the risk that's always there when electricity ventures into the outside world.

Numerous proprietary kits containing all you need to install fancy fairy lights for your trees, practical bollard lights or lanterns to define a path or driveway, are available from garden centres and some hardware and DIY stores. Although installation details vary from make to make, the basic principles are the same: a step-down transformer is used to reduce the current rating from the mains to a level that's safe — you wouldn't receive a fatal shock if you accidentally touched the cores.

Setting up the transformer

The transformer is typically a fairly small unit, which wouldn't be conspicuous housed in a cupboard in the house, utility room or outbuilding. It's simply plugged into a 13A socket outlet. It's a good idea to fit a special RCD socket outlet in place of the ordinary one, as this will trip the supply and switch it off if there's any damage to the cable or fittings.

The type of transformer you need depends on the number of lights you want to power: the manufacturer will tell you this. The cable is simply stripped and connected to the transformer's screw-down pillar terminals.

Choosing the correct cable

Thicker cable is needed for low-voltage lighting set-ups — a 40W bulb running at 12 volts will take up 3.3A, compared with the 0.16A it would take at mains 240 volts.

With many kits, the cable is the two-core PVC-sheathed type and is connected to the lamp terminals with ingenious terminal spikes. The cable is simply located over two metal pins inside a covered connection chamber and pressed into place: the spikes pierce the insulation and make the connections without the need to strip the sheathing or prepare the cores. This may also make the connection to the lampholder itself or you have to attach leads from the lampholder to the terminal spike chamber.

Many fittings include ground spikes, which you simply push into the earth to secure the light. Festoon lights such as those illustrated on the right suspend a row of fairy bulbs on the cable, often using spike connections, and these can be strung up in trees or along walls for a colourful, festive effect which is just right for a party or barbeque.

Routing the cable

There's no need to bury the low-voltage cable underground due to its safety in use, but trailing cables can look untidy and the nuisance that would result in accidentally damaging the cable with garden tools makes it sensible to dig a trench for it. Enclose the cable in conduit to prevent damage when deep-digging.

1. *Low voltage lighting comes in kits containing bulb holders and cable connectors for easy installation*

2. *The low voltage cable can be simply pressed into the bulb holder without the need to strip the cores*

3. *When the cap is fitted, integral terminal pins pierce the cable and make the electrical connection*

4. *You can suspend rows of low voltage light bulbs on a single cable, creating decorative colourful strings*

CHAPTER 7

Lighting choice

Choosing the right fittings for your lighting arrangements is fraught with confusion — there's an overwhelmingly massive selection to choose from, and although much relies on personal preference, it's important to choose the fitting that's going to give both the effect you want and the best means of installing it in your electrical system. But most large store lighting departments should be able to help: they've a vast range of decorative, practical and stylish products which offer you plenty of scope. Whether it's the classical look of brass fittings and delicate shades in etched glass, the streamlined modernistic approach offered by fittings in primary colours with bright and breezy adornments, or the rustic charm of whittled wood, you will be sure to find just what you want. And not only will you be able to furnish yourself with the light fittings that you need, but also you will find all the accessories vital to the installation — from bulbs to socket outlets; fuse wire to cable and flex.

TO SUIT YOUR DECOR . . .

Table lamps and bedside lamps fulfil a function, but they should also complement the style of your room decor. Stores offer both classical and modern styles of lampshades ready-made to fit specific bodies or which can be mixed-and-matched to suit your tastes. Fabric shades complement soft furnishings, while glass bowls and oil-lamp style fittings with brass bodies lend a period air. Stiffened fabric and geometric patterns give a modern look.

PRACTICAL AND PURPOSEFUL . . .
Where you need a clear light to see by — in the kitchen or bathroom, for instance — opt for fluorescent tubes fitted with diffusers, which cast no harsh shadows, or spotlights on tracks or clusters for directing a beam just when it's needed: stores have a range of fittings — inconspicuous or brazen — in various finishes to give your schemes the benefit of utility lighting with a decorative accent.

LIGHT THE NIGHT AIR . . .

Lighting the outside of your house is just as important as illuminating the interior — both to deter burglars and to provide a bright welcome for visitors — and most stores sell a selection of traditional lantern-style fittings and utilitarian bulkheads that fit the bill perfectly. To light the approach to your house, consider spotlights on ground spikes, and where you need a roving beam, there are clip-on inspection lamps to oblige.

BRIGHT LIGHTS FOR KIDS . . .
Children like bright, colourful decor and lights and lampshades can be a source of amusement and interest. Most stores have a range of fittings in bold primary colours and designs ranging from cartoon characters to abstract patterns that are sure to please. And when the kids grow older and need a light to see their homework by, you'll find the theme continued with a selection of dainty desk lamps.

Index

ARTWORK
Hayward Art Group

PHOTOGRAPHY:
Paul Beattie: 13
The Camden Studio: 17
Dave King: 19
Steve Tanner: 31
Elizabeth Whiting & Associates: 8, 10 (tl), 18
All other pictures: Malcolm Pendrill